How to Quilting for Beginners: The Complete Easy Guide to Learn Quilting Quickly

Annie Ramsey

PUBLISHED BY:

Annie Ramsey

Copyright © 2015

Visit our website to get more books information:

justhappyforever.com

All rights reserved.

No part of this publication may be copied, reproduced in any format, by any means, electronic or otherwise, without prior consent from the copyright owner and publisher of this book.

Disclaimer

The information contained in this ebook is for general information purposes only. The information is provided by the authors and while we endeavor to keep the information up to date and correct, we make no representations or warranties of any kind, express or implied, about the completeness, accuracy, reliability, suitability or availability with respect to the ebook or the information, products, services, or related graphics contained in the ebook for any purpose. Any reliance you place on such information is therefore strictly at your own risk.

WAIT! Before you continue…

Just to say thank you for purchasing this book, I want to give you a 100% FREE GIFT (valued at $5.99): *10 Hot Tips for Eating Right & Losing Weight Fast.*

You will get the tips for eating right and losing weight fast to make you health.

Click here to access your Free gift

Table of Contents

Introduction

Chapter 1: Let's Talk a Little about History

Chapter 2: Getting Started!

- Let Me Introduce Your Tools
- Tips for Newbies
- Choosing a Project

Chapter 3: Important Things to Understand

- The Basics
- The Quilt Block
- Squares and Rectangles
- Triangles, Diamonds, and Hexagons

Chapter 4: Designing Your First Project

Chapter 5: Fabric Preparation and Cutting

Making Your Templates

Chapter 6: Piecing a Block

Finishing the Quilt Top

Chapter 7: Making Your Quilt Sandwich

Chapter 8: Tying and Quilting

Tying a Quilt

Quilting Lines

Chapter 9: Binding Your Edges

Making binding

Attaching the binding

Chapter 10: Finishing Your Project

Chapter 11: Project 1- Modern Placemat Walk-Through

Chapter 12: Project 2- T-Shirt Quilt Walk-Through

Chapter 13: Some Special Projects

Rag Quilts

Puff Quilt

Trapunto

Hanging Sleeves

Chapter 14: Two Alternative Piecing Methods

English Paper Piecing

Foundation Piecing

Chapter 15: More Common Quilting Terms

Conclusion

Introduction

Welcome to the rich and amazing world of quilting! And congratulations for deciding to learn it. That is an excellent choice. This amazing, addictive craft will soon fill your life with joy and colors, with creativity and exhilaration.

This book contains proven steps and strategies on how to make your first quilt and provides the bases for learning the basics of quilting. The steps and information written in this book are universal and easy to understand for beginners. The book includes the description of errors which quilters might make and their easy solutions are recommended. This book will aid you in evading the mistakes and learn from the experience of other quilters. The basic equipment, tool and skill for beginner and intermediate quilters mentioned in this book will help you in achieving the maximum out of your efforts.

If you are a house wife, and entrepreneur or someone who wants to learn the art of quilting for pastime activities or starting a business, the surely this book will serve as a guiding star for you.

Quilting is as varied and creative as the millions of people who quilt. Every quilt is unique, and so is every quilter. There are no 'rules' for quilting; there's really no right or wrong way to do things. It's an ancient traditional craft that is still innovative, fresh, and constantly changing with the times. From Buenos Aires to Beijing to Belfast, you'll find quilters, quilts, and an astonishing array of color and creativity.

Meant both as a step-by-step introduction to quilting and as a reference tool, this guide will help you get your foot on the ladder and hopefully avoid most of the usual beginner's mistakes.

And then you will be ready to take your first steps alone on the path of your new life, a life we hope will be filled with projects, new techniques, new patterns, tons of fabrics and hours of bliss.

Chapter 1: Let's Talk a Little about History

Modern quilting combines two truly ancient crafts, quilting and piecing. The oldest known quilted piece, the center section of a floor covering, was found in Mongolia and dates back to the first century. However, there are drawings and references to quilted items going back to the ancient Egyptians circa 3000 BC. Most early quilting was used to create garments for protection and/or warmth, depending on the climate. Crusaders returning to their homes in Europe brought quilted items back with them, sparking an interest in the craft. Quilted items were first used as padding garments under armor for both knights and their horses and, later on, became fashionable for coats and doublets.

Quilts as bedding was actually a 'late' idea in the history of quilting, and it was the provenance of the upper class. These were called 'whole cloth' quilts, made from a single large piece of fabric (no patchwork) stitched to another large piece, with wool in between. Only the wealthy could afford such fabric, and only they had the time to sit and do all that hand stitching. Many designs sewn on the quilts were complex and beautiful; their purpose was simply to keep the stuffing from shifting around. Practicality made into art. Quilting designs still range from simple straight lines to intricate swirls, curls, figures, and vines.

When the European settlers came to the New World, they brought their quilting skills with them. Fabric, however, could be hard to come by in the colonies, particularly as settlers moved west, away from the shipping centers on the eastern coasts. Enter another ancient craft --- piecing. Piecing smaller bits together to make something large enough to use simply must date back to the earliest cavemen. It's only logical when survival is challenging and materials scarce. Many of the early settlers in the Americas were also battling for their survival, and they couldn't move west to claim land from the wilderness dragging looms with them, nor did they have the time or space to do much weaving. So they used their ingenuity and recycled what they had. The scrap bits from bought fabric and the small good patches left in otherwise worn-out and un-wearable clothes were saved and pieced together for quilt tops --- and patchwork quilts were suddenly everywhere. It didn't take long before quilters began arranging the colors into pleasing patterns.

Hand-quilting a bed covering, however, was very time-consuming and took up a lot of space (it still is and does). So, many women would do the piecing during the long winters that kept them indoors. When spring came and the animals could be turned out into the fields, the quilting frame could be set up in the barn. Later, the 'quilting bee' was born --- women gathering and working together to quilt the tops they'd pieced during the winter. With the quilting frames set up outdoors, the women could share the work, swap ideas and techniques, and socialize. They could also finish many quilts in a day, as well as teach the young ones how to do it. Followed by a dinner gathering of all the families, with music and dancing afterwards, quilting bees became quite a welcome social event for everyone.

Every ethnic group has brought its own patterns, colors schemes, techniques, and stories into quilting. It's truly international. Historic events, local legends, and much-loved people and pets have all found their way into quilt patterns. Perhaps you'll create your own story through a quilt.

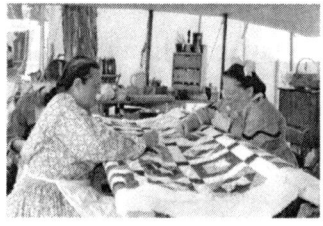

Women quilting on a floor frame. Image from Flicker by Francis

Chapter 2: Getting Started!

Let Me Introduce Your Tools

The tools you need to get started are actually very few; the tools available to you are numerous. Until you know what area of the process you enjoy the most, it's best to keep your equipment minimal. You may already have the basic things you need to start quilting, and they're all useful for other purposes if you decide that quilting is not for you. It's very easy in crafting of any kind to invest a lot of money into all sorts of equipment at the start, when you're all gung-ho and excited to create, only to end up with a closet full of stuff you never really use.

So, what are those few tools? Sewing needles, pins, thread, scissors, an iron, a ruler, pencil/pen, a stitch-ripper, fabric, quilting pens, some old poster board or thin cardboard, and, maybe, a thimble. Really, that's it! All the other stuff in the store is 'bells and whistles', things to make the crafting go quicker or easier (perhaps), and I'll discuss a few of them in the more detailed sections. I said that 'perhaps' because some of the fancier items have a learning curve of their own, which could slow you way down while you master the tool. You can always pick them up later, if they appeal to both you and your budget.

Of course, you also need a very basic knowledge of sewing. If you don't have that already, God bless you but, please, gently set this book aside and go learn. YouTube has some wonderful instructional videos. You don't need to be good, but you do need to know a few sewing basics. Then, come back and learn to quilt, OK? You'll thank me for this.

If you have a basic sewing kit, you're more than halfway there right now. The most expensive item on the list is a good pair of scissors to be used on nothing except fabric. I repeat, cut only fabric with them. Cutting *anything else* with them will dull them really fast and ruin them for using on fabric. If you want to splurge, this is the item to put your money into. Even if you decide to try a rotary cutter later on, you'll still need a good pair of scissors exclusively for fabric.

The most unfamiliar item on the list is probably the quilting pens, or fabric marking pens. These usually come two or three to a package and are inexpensive. They're markers made especially for quilting that don't stain fabric, and you'll use them to mark the cutting and/or sewing lines on your fabric pieces. A package usually has both dark and light colored ones in it, so you can choose the one that will show up best on the different colors you'll be using. You can always wait until you've chosen your fabrics before picking these up so you'll know what color(s) you'll need. I wouldn't advise trying to substitute regular washable markers. It's just not worth taking the chance of ruining your fabric.

The poster board/cardboard can definitely be a recycled piece; actually empty cereal boxes are good. It'll be used to make the cutting templates for your pieces, which you'll cut using your *other* scissors, those household ones, *not* your sewing scissors. The stitch-ripper gets a workout from even seasoned quilters, so make sure you have one. The thimble is up to you, but personally I always struggle with using one.

Tips for Newbies

1. Curb your ambition. Start with a small manageable project like a pillow or placemat. Your first quilting project is a practice piece, a learning activity. Choose something you can finish is a reasonable amount of time with the skills currently at your disposal. As your skills grow, so can your ambition.

2. Choose a pattern using large pieces that are square or rectangular. They're easier to sew and the project will go quicker. Finishing your first project and having it look okay is tremendous encouragement to continue working and learning this craft.

3. Seriously consider using pre-cut fabric or even a quilt kit. Master the piecing and quilting this time, and you can tackle the cutting challenges with more confidence later .

4. Learn the terms as you encounter them. Look them up or ask a quilter if you're unsure what they mean. You need to learn to 'talk the talk'.

5. Take it slowly. Read instructions carefully and understand each step thoroughly *before* you start it. Going off half-cocked can cost you a lot in time and frustration later.

6. Get help or advice when you need it. The Internet is a great resource, so use it. Ask friends, family, or the employees in craft stores. Find a local quilting group. Don't be embarrassed to ask.

7. Expect setbacks and stay realistic. Don't beat yourself up over 'silly' mistakes --- even seasoned veterans make them! That's why you bought that stitch-ripper!

8. Be kind to yourself. You know that no one's perfect, so don't think you should be.

9. There are no mistakes, only learning experiences! Remember the words of the great Thomas Edison, an inventor of truly genius proportions, "I have not failed. I've just found 10,000 ways that won't work."

Choosing a Project

YOU are the most important factor when choosing your first project: your current skill level and your interests. There are many different skills involved in a quilting project, and you need to honestly assess where your strengths, weaknesses, and interest in learning lie. Then you can play to your strengths and have a much more pleasant first experience.

Sewing skills are obviously the first factor. Novices should stick with long straight lines and simple quilting techniques. Those who are more experienced can get a little more adventurous. Machine-sewn rag quilts are a nice choice for beginners who can use a machine, and I'll give you instructions for one of those in a later chapter. Have you done any hand sewing? Do you like it? Then hand-quilting a pattern on a solid fabric might be just right for you. If the whole sewing aspect is not up your alley, you'll want a project that is minimal in that respect, such as a placemat.

If you love colors, patterns, and shapes, then design may be your strength. Go with a simple project, but make it pop with your arrangement of the pieces or your color combinations. Some very impressive pieces are simple in construction but require an artistic eye to make them work. You may need a slightly larger piece to showcase your design skills, such as a table runner or crib quilt.

Cutting and piecing are the areas for very detail oriented people or puzzle-solvers. If measuring and precision are your strengths, you can tackle a more intricate design or even a smaller scale project like a cell phone case. Those little areas may be just the kind of challenge you'll relish, or perhaps a crib quilt with small pieces is a better fit for you.

Lastly, ask yourself just how many new things you want to learn how to do for your first project. If everything's new to you, keep your project really simple, learn each skill, and discover what you like. Talking with quilters can be a revelation. Many of them hate some aspects of quilting. Really! They keep learning, and they choose patterns and projects that challenge them in their favorite areas. They'll keep the other aspects rather simple.

The important thing is to choose a project that you'll actually finish. That's why somewhat small and simple is best. You'll end up with a finished item that looks good, and not a partially completed 'thing' that radiates guilt at you from the back corner of your sewing table and haunts your sleep. Finishing one quilted block is really good, and it easily can be made into a placemat, pillow, or wall hanging. Many a beginner has foundered with 'too big, too complicated' because they fell in love with a picture. Save the king-sized Dresden Plate bed quilt for much later. Start modestly and you'll be successful.

As we go through the steps in creating a quilted project, you'll see many options that can help you maximize your strengths and minimize your weaknesses. Let these help you choose a project that will be enjoyable for you, so you can handle the challenges and be eager for your second project! In a later chapter, I'll walk you through making a striking but simple placemat that's a perfect first project for the beginning quilter and also a popular and fun type of quilt made with old t-shirts.

Chapter 3: Important Things to Understand

The Basics

Before we tackle making a quilt, you need to become familiar with some of the jargon. Every craft, like every job, has its own set of terms that make talking about it easier, a sort of verbal shorthand. So, now it's time to learn to speak quilting!

First off, a quilt is made with 4 basic pieces:

- Quilt top: the top layer that can be pieced, appliquéd, embroidered, or made of one solid piece

- Batting: the middle layer of padding

- Backing: the bottom layer, traditionally one large piece of fabric

- Binding: a piece that covers the raw edges once the layers are put together

Unless it's a whole cloth solid piece, the quilt top is created from quilt blocks. Each block in a particular quilt is usually the same size. There are many different traditional quilt block patterns to chose from, and they can be alternated with solid pieces or just all connected together. Once the individual blocks are sewn together, they're arranged and joined to form the quilt top. When the top, batting, and backing are layered together, the whole thing is referred to as the quilt sandwich. This is when the actual quilting is done. Quilting is the sewing that holds the sandwich together and prevents the batting from shifting around and getting lumpy when the finished quilt is used or washed. It ranges from simply tying knots to very ornate hand-stitched patterns. Once that's finished, the binding is sewn around the cut edges to finish it all off. A style of quilt called a rag quilt, great for beginners, isn't bound at all. All of the seams on a rag quilt are purposely left exposed so they'll fray into that raggedy look.

The other odd words you'll hear from quilters (and see on their web sites) are mostly about fabric. Piecing a quilt top requires a lot of smallish amounts of cloth, which means lugging a lot of cloth bolts over to the cutting counter in the fabric store. Later some employee will need to wrestle the bolts back to their original spots. To simplify this process for everyone, many fabric stores have pre-cut lengths of fabric available, which have become known as fat eighths and fat quarters. Pre-cut fabric in common shapes and sizes has also become a popular time-saver, and the packages of these have their own whimsical names such as layer cakes, jelly rolls, or honeybuns. If you don't like measuring and precision cutting, you'll learn your way around these terms very quickly!

The Quilt Block

Your quilt block is the starting point for your project, and there are very many options, far too many to show you here. Browse the quilting sites on the web and you'll see a wonderful variety of block patterns, many of them free to print, or you can easily sketch out your own on paper. We'll just look at the basics here. Some block patterns are much more difficult than others because of the size or shape of the pieces. A great beginner's project is to make only one or two quilt blocks that can be easily converted into placemats, table runners, pillow shams, or throw pillows. The crazily ambitious can make a sampler quilt with each block done in a different pattern.

Squares and Rectangles

This is the shape for beginners, and it's for a very good reason. They're cut on the straight grain of the material, the direction it's been woven. This makes them stable in shape and size. Cutting across the grain creates what's called the bias, and it stretches. Of course, you remember that all the pieces have to fit together at the end, right? Working with bias cuts makes that more difficult. However, you'll find lots of patterns that are built around basic squares and rectangles that are beautiful. Basic four-patch and nine-patch are where most new quilters start. Take a look at these three quilts, all made from simple squares

They look wildly different, but it's due to the color and fabric choices. Really, that's the only difference! Image from Flicker by Frederick

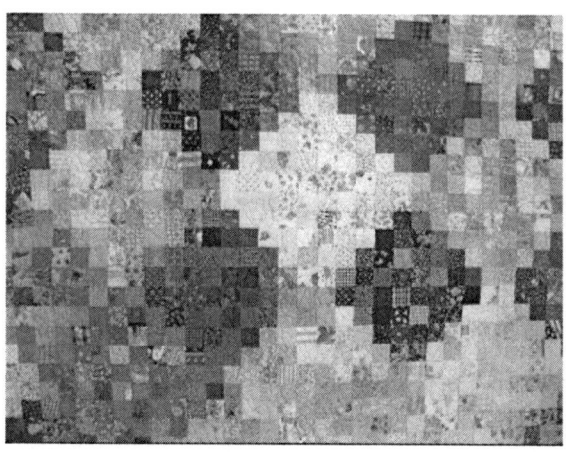

Choosing different color schemes and arrangements can make the finished quilts look completely different. Image from Flicker by Jimson

The other easy way for beginners to make a simple block look much more complex is to use a technique called quick piecing. Image from Flicker by Jason

This uses extra-large squares that are sewn together, with the nine-patch being a particularly good choice. Then you cut the huge square in half both ways, making four smaller squares called daughters. The daughter squares, which each now have both large and squares as well as rectangles, can be rotated in different directions and put back together to produce many patterns from that one big pieced square. This process really is simple, but it easier to see if you actually do it.

Get some paper and some colored markers or crayons. Draw a large 3 X 3-square grid; then color in the nine resulting squares using different colors and designs such as dots. Grab your household scissors and cut your grid into four equal sized squares, right up the middle. See how the shapes have changed? Make another one using different colors and do the same. Now you have eight squares. Sit and rotate them around, move them, mix them up, and put them back together into one big square, and you'll understand the beauty of quick piecing. It's a great technique for beginners, and it's particularly well suited for machine sewing because you're working with larger pieces.

Triangles, Diamonds, and Hexagons

These are the simplest bias-edged pieces to work with. If you're an experienced sewer, using a block with triangles is worth consideration, particularly right triangles that have only one bias cut. That's what's used in the classic Pinwheel design shown here.

Pinwheel Block

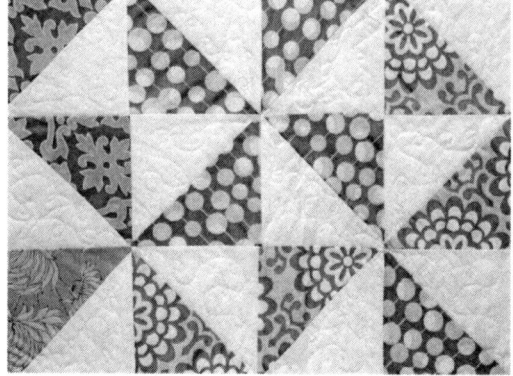

Wide diamonds can be cut with only two bias edges. They can be used to create optical illusions with the right color arrangement, and are often used to create crib quilts in a pattern frequently called

Baby Blocks. You can get a lovely 3D effect as you can see. Image from Flicker by Thomas

Tumbling Blocks

Hexagons have four bias cuts and are a little trickier to work with. They produce a great end result, however, as you can see in this popular Grandmother's Flower Garden design, made completely with hexagons. Image from Flicker by Grinder

Grandmother's Flower Garden

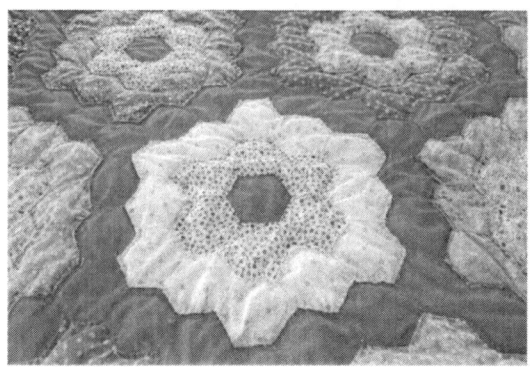

These, as well as any other odd shape you'd like to name, are best left for the future. Image from Flicker by berry45

Circles and More

Circles are a very advanced shape to try to work with, as are skinny diamonds. There is a special technique for bringing them into more intermediate reach, called foundation or paper piecing, which I'll discuss a little later. The finished quilts are fantastic, as you'll see when you look at quilt blocks on the web, but the construction is definitely challenging. Quilts made completely from 'odd' shapes, rather than pattern blocks, are called Crazy Quilts. They're like wonderful abstract paintings, as you can see.

Crazy Quilt

So the time has come. Browse through quilting books or magazines at your local fabric store. Check out the many quilting sites on the Internet. Design your own quilt block from quick piecing or on graph paper. It's time to choose a pattern. Unless you have a lot of sewing experience, stick with a pattern using squares and rectangles. Image from Flicker by Fredie

You'll 'ooh' and 'aah' over some of the quilts you'll see, but be realistic. Start with a block that uses larger pieces. Remember, you have to sew all those pieces together! You have a lifetime of quilting ahead to tackle the more intricate patterns.

Chapter 4: Designing Your First Project

Now that you've chosen your quilt block, you must choose your project. There are a number of reasonable options for a beginner, and your skill level should guide your choice. A large single quilt block makes a beautiful placemat, pot holder/hot pad, wall hanging, or throw pillow. Two together can make a pillow sham, and three or four join up into a table runner. Add a few more for a crib quilt/lap throw. I really wouldn't go any larger than that to start your quilting adventure. As I've said before, many a beginner has been lost to 'too big, too complicated'.

Pick a project and decide on the finished size. It's easiest to start with complete instructions for a project, telling you the block size, finished size, and how much fabric you'll need. Otherwise, you're going to have to measure and figure it out. Many people sketch out their plan on paper, just like we did with the quick piecing. Graph paper is particularly helpful here with guiding you in design, particularly with color placement. A design sketch can help you get the finished piece assembled in the correct layout.

Color

There are several ways to choose your colors, but they should be compatible with your project's function and intended surroundings. If you're working from a pattern you like, just plan on the same colors they've used, if that works for you, or do simple substitutions for the same look. However, as you saw earlier with the basic squares quilts, you can do a lot with colors and prints to make your project uniquely yours.

You can go monotone for an understated look with graduated shades of the same color; or you can play with tone like the muted nine-patch you saw earlier, using all plain soft colors in closely related shades. You can do a gradient arrangement of shades from light to dark, or an arrangement by intensity for that optical illusion that you saw in the Baby Blocks. You can plan to mix patterns with solids, which works so well in the classic Pinwheel. You can go for contrast by putting opposing colors together, mix patterns with patterns, prints with solids, make it completely random ... you can use color and pattern however you like. You do, however, need to *plan* what you're going to do so that you can buy the correct amount of fabric.

Fabric

Quilts can be made from anything, but most are made using 100% cotton fabric. That's mostly what you'll find at the fabric store in the quilting section as well as online. Cotton fabrics are the easiest to sew, the most durable, and they absorb moisture. They also crease well, which makes piecing and ironing easier. Blends don't shrink or fade, but they also are harder to press and they're stiffer, making them more difficult to quilt, especially by hand. Never mix the two in one quilt top, so if you're planning on using up fabric scraps make sure they're all the same material, either blend or all cotton.

When choosing printed fabric, it's important to know two things about patterns: direction and scale. Some material has a print that goes in a specific direction. These will require buying extra fabric to get your cut pieces all going the same direction as the print. Fold the printed fabric both directions to check for this if you're not sure, or ask the sales clerk if it's a directional print. Some are obvious, but others can be a little trickier. Scale is the size of the actual print. Does it have large figures on it or small? How will it look cut up into the shapes you want? Will the pattern, colors, or motif get lost when you cut it up?

The last thing you need to think about is the backing fabric. This can be pieced or patch worked, but for your first project, you probably don't want to fuss with that. I'd recommend using one single piece of fabric, which can be either plain or printed. You'll need to decide the color and size for this piece of your quilt, and you'll need to add a few inches in both directions to get it to fit well with your quilt top piece later. If you're making a pillow or sham, you'll need two pieces of backing, muslin (which won't show) for the backing of your quilted piece and cotton (which will show) to make the actual pillow back.

Remember, if you want to keep cutting to a minimum, look for the pre-cut pieces. You can buy long strips to cut squares or triangles off of, or you can buy completely pre-cut shapes. Make sure you've decided how much fabric you need in each color and pattern that you've chosen before you head to the store. The clerks there should be glad to help you find what you need, give you advice (wanted or unwanted), and generally guide you in choosing your materials.

You'll also need thread that blends with your chosen colors. Get high quality cotton thread or cotton-covered polyester. Regular inexpensive polyester thread can actually cut your fabric. If you're using a set palette of colors, you can simply choose thread to match. If you're mixing a number of colors, then a dark gray is a great color for dark fabrics, and off-white for the lighter ones.

If you don't want to make your own cutting templates from cardboard, then buy some sheets of template plastic or some pre-cut templates now, along with any other little things you may still need. Don't let the clerk talk you into expensive 'bells and whistles' though!

Chapter 5: Fabric Preparation and Cutting

There's great debate among quilters about pre-washing fabrics, with experts in both camps. Let me sum up the disagreement for you. Cotton fabric can shrink, even if it's labeled pre-shrunk, and the color can run, even if it's labeled colorfast. Pre-washing takes care of both these things before you measure and cut. It also removes the sizing, which is what makes unwashed fabric stiffer. The anti-pre-washers want the sizing left in, particularly if they machine quilt. They say the fabric is easier to work with at every stage. Any shrinkage later will just help hide the stitches. Personally, I'm a pre-washer, but you're in good company whichever way you choose to go.

If you pre-wash, use a mild detergent. You may need to iron your fabric nice and smooth afterwards to make it easier to measure and cut your pieces. You can also use a little spray starch to get some of the stiffness back in. If you don't pre-wash your fabrics, expect a little shrinkage when you wash your finished quilt. This will give it the slightly wrinkly puckered look that you see on antique quilts. Some people love this; some hate it. If you use blended cottons, you won't really have this problem but remember that blends are more difficult to piece and quilt ... and around it goes!

The next step is to make your templates. If you bought templates, skip to the next section. If you bought pre-cut shapes, you can skip to the next chapter. You can use any light cardboard like cereal boxes, tissue boxes, or the bits that come in new clothes. You can also use the clear plastic snap-on lids that come with many food containers, like margarine or coffee. You'll need your household scissors, a pen or pencil, a ruler, and your pattern for your quilt block. If you've downloaded a pattern, you should be able to print it from your computer. Make sure to check your printer settings, however. Many printers are set to 'shrink to page' and that will throw all the sizes off. Go into those settings and uncheck that box. You want it to print 'actual size'. Those printed pieces are what you'll use to cut your templates and they need to be correct! If you're using squares, rectangles, or triangles, then making templates is nice and easy.

Making Your Templates

You can make your own templates easily, and for some patterns you'll need to make them, so it's good to learn how to do it. You may use either thin cardboard or poster board or purchased template plastic that is available in sheets at the fabric store. The process is the same whichever you choose to use. Plastic is more durable, and you won't need to cut as many templates, but for a first project in particular, cardboard is fine.

First you need to cut out your pattern pieces, and you probably don't want to cut up a magazine if that's where you've found your block pattern. Some patterns also need to be enlarged before using. Check this carefully since many magazines, books, and web sites will give you small versions of each piece. You'll need to enlarge them before printing. Most people either photocopy or print out the pattern; then you'll just cut out all those pieces. Trace your patterns onto the cardboard [unprinted side] or the plastic. Fine-tipped markers are fine for this, and use a ruler when tracing straight edges. Exactness is important so your pieces will all fit together correctly.

Next you need to check whether your pattern shows the cutting line or the sewing line. Patterns vary on this so you need to look carefully or your pieces will not be the correct size! If it's the cutting line, then use your ruler to mark a line running one-quarter inch *inside* the line. If it's the sewing line, mark a new line one-quarter inch *outside* the pattern line. In either case you'll have two pattern shapes, one being a quarter-inch larger than the other. This gives you both a sewing line and a cutting line to follow. Next, cut out your templates using a small pair of sharp scissors. Finally, carefully cut out the center of your template. You should end up with a hollow piece with a quarter-inch wide edge. If you've used cardboard, you'll need to cut several identical templates for each piece because the edges will get worn with use, making your measurements less exact. Find a plastic bag or envelope to store your templates for this project, and label it with the pattern name.

Finished Templates Examples 1 and 2. Image from Flicker by Terry45

Cutting

Make sure your fabric is ready and you have a large stable worktop. Also determine how many pieces you need of each shape. You want to cut all your pieces at one time. What you're going to be doing is fairly simple: tracing your templates onto your fabric, and then cutting the pieces out. We're going to be using scissors for this, although most quilters nowadays use a rotary cutter and cutting mat. The equipment for rotary cutting is a little pricey, and you need to learn to use it properly. If you decide you want to do more quilting, you can go online or to a craft store and learn how to do this later. For now, scissors are fine.

There's one last thing you'll need to know before tracing and cutting your pieces, and that's about fabric grain. Some of your pattern pieces may indicate grain lines, and you need to pay close attention to these. Fabric is woven with threads going in both crosswise and lengthwise directions, and the threads cross each other at right angles. Crosswise threads have just a little stretch to them; lengthwise threads don't. If you cut across the grain, you've made a bias cut, which stretches a lot. Little arrows on the pattern pieces indicate how to line that piece up with the lengthwise grain, and you should mark them on your templates. You'll need to put your template onto the fabric with the arrows following the lengthwise grain.

Paying attention to the grain lines, place your templates on the fabric and hold firmly in place. Then use your washable fabric markers to trace around both the outside and the inside of your fabric, marking both your cutting and sewing lines carefully. If you find it easier, make a series of small dots instead of a solid line. Practice on some old fabric or paper before you use your 'good' stuff. Take it slowly and, please, don't try to use a pencil. It doesn't wash out of some fabrics! After a few trial runs, you'll figure out the most comfortable arrangement of hands, marker, and fabric for you.

When you're ready to mark your fabric, remember to trace onto the wrong side of the material. That's the underside that's usually less intense in color (or even lacking color) on cottons. The right side is the top part that you'll see in the finished quilt. Even though your markings should be washable, you don't want them on the right side of the fabric. When we get to the sewing, knowing the right and wrong sides of the fabric is important. So, trace your templates onto the wrong side of the fabric. Then use your sewing scissors to carefully cut around the cutting line on each one. Keep count as you go. You may find it easier to make little stacks of each color or print. Check your template edges periodically, especially if they're cardboard, and move to a new one if they look even a little worn. You'll end up with a whole lot of cut fabric pieces! Stash each stack into a zip-lock baggie. Measure twice, cut once, and make sure to keep an accurate count, although you may want to cut one or two extras.

Cutting quilt pieces using a ruler and a rotary blade. Image from Flicker by Oliver

You've just completed the first major step in quilting! You're ready to put your project together. Congratulations!

Chapter 6: Piecing a Block

Now it's time to put your pieces together, either by hand or machine. First you'll need to practice, using some fabric scraps, so that you can sew a quarter-inch seam. If you're working on a sewing machine and having difficulty, check online for tips on machine piecing with your particular sewing machine. You shouldn't have any major problems if you're hand sewing. Get comfortable with these small seams before you go any further.

You'll need to lay out your pieces to be sure you know where each color and print is going to go. If you have more than one quilt block in your project, this is imperative. On top of a bed or on the floor is perfectly fine for this. You want to make sure you know what's going where in each quilt block. Stand back and look at the balance of color. Rearrange your pieces until you're satisfied. This is your final check on your design, and you may want to bring in a second opinion. Sometimes others can see an imbalance that we can't. It's also a good idea to sketch out your final plan so you can refer to it later when you're assembling the block. Once you're happy with your arrangement, it's time to start sewing.

Whether you're working by hand or by machine, assembling a quilt block follows the same procedure. Basically, you start in the center of the block and work outwards, adding each piece as it comes along. Although it sounds very simple, there are some things to look out for along the way.

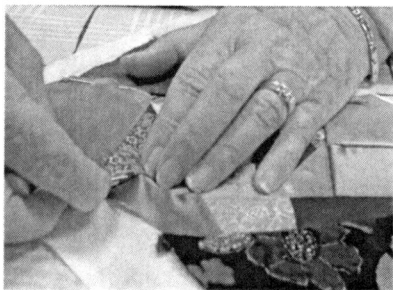

Piecing by hand. Image from Flicker by Gerald

Pressing

You'll need to press your seams as you go along to make assembling the pieces easier. First you'll simply set the stitching by pressing the piece just as you've sewn it, making the stitching nice and flat. Then you'll open it up and press your seam to one side. It doesn't matter if you go seam left, seam right, or open seam like a butterfly. Many quilters prefer pressing the seams open, half to each side, because this eliminates bulky layers, particularly when it comes to quilting them later on. What really matters is that all your seams in the block or blocks go the same way. If you have a light piece next to a dark piece, always press toward the dark so it doesn't show through the lighter piece. This really helps you when you're putting it together.

You also want to remember to press, not iron. Don't move the iron around, even on long seams --- just press it on your seam and lift it up. Sliding the iron along will stretch your pieced block out of shape. Good pressing will make assembling and quilting easier later.

Assembling the Block

Pieces are connected by putting the right sides together and sewing along that sewing line that you marked earlier. That sounds super simple, but anyone who's done this can tell you that they've goofed this up several times (at least). It can be very easy to get the sides of the material mixed up and stitch the right side of one piece to the wrong side of the other, or end up with the wrong sides facing each other instead of the right sides. Mr. Stitch-Ripper comes to your rescue when this happens. Carefully remove the stitching and start again, knowing that we've all been there many times and that you are not alone.

The other thing that sounds super easy (but can actually be tricky) is to make sure your prints are going the same way, especially if you're using a directional print. If you're making two blocks, you really need to check this carefully because your finished blocks will look strange next to each other if one print goes up and in the next block the same print goes down or sideways.

If you're following pattern instructions, they should tell you where to start, but let's walk through this with a simple nine-patch.

First you'll put the right sides of A and B together and sew a one-quarter inch seam along your marked sewing line. Then you'll open them out and put the right sides of B and C together. Sew that seam and then press the two seams before continuing. If you're doing two or more blocks, you can 'assembly line' by repeating this row on your other blocks right now. Then you can press them all at once. You'll need to keep them separated by which row belongs to which block, so plastic baggies and sticky notes can come in handy. Pop each piece back in its bag to keep things straight. Whether you assemble a block at a time or block section at a time is up to you.

Once your seams are pressed, you'll repeat the whole process for D, E, and F. Pieces G, H, and I will be handled the same. When all three rows are sewn and pressed, place the right side of ABC on the right side of DEF and stitch and press. Finally repeat with the right side of ABC on the right side of GHI. Your finished block should end up with DAG as the first column on the left. Check it. If you are looking at some other combination of letters right now, you got the right and left sides swapped around when you pieced them. I warned you that it's easy to do! The process is fairly straightforward, but now maybe you can see why keeping the right and left sides in the correct places can get confusing. Keep your sketched plan handy. Just when you're feeling all puffed with yourself and thinking 'this is easy", you'll look down and see that you've put a piece in sideways or upside down. The great quilting gods keep us humble. Welcome to the sisterhood!

If you really want to practice first, draw some colored squares on paper. Staple your rows together and fold the 'seams' to the side. It can help you see how to match up your rows and to devise your own system for keeping things straight. Use up some scrap fabric practicing.

As you go along, continually check your seam size. [There are nifty little adjustable rulers you can get inexpensively for this.] Having your sewing lines marked helps keep your seams correct, but check and measure anyway. You need your sewn pieces to be the correct size in order to fit all the bits together at the end, and incorrect or crooked seams will trip you up. Just a tiny $1/16^{th}$ off the correct seam allowance can add up to a half inch later.

Quick Piecing

If you're doing quick piecing, you've used large squares to create this block. The next step would be to make your daughter blocks. Measure and cut straight up the middle of EBH, ending up with two pieces. Then divide each of those halves evenly along ABC. This should leave you with four blocks the same size.

Each block has a large square, two rectangles, and a small square. You can move them around and stitch them back together, or set them aside to mix with the daughter blocks from another large block later.

Set-in or Y-Seams

If you've used anything except squares or rectangles, you'll need to learn to do a Y-seam, properly called a set-in seam, in order to assemble the block. I was surprised when I found out that many quilters are afraid of these! They are a little easier to hand sew than they are on a machine, but a little planning and knowledge can make them a piece of cake. So, let's tackle the 'dreaded Y-seam'!

First, these involve bias edges that stretch. Handle the pieces carefully before and during sewing to avoid stretching them at all. On a y-seam, it's also important to remember that *you will never sew into the seam allowance*, not even a little bit. Therefore, it's necessary to mark where your seams will begin and end on each piece. If you've marked your sewing lines, then you've got this already. If you haven't, use your ruler and mark the intersections of the quarter-inch seams with a dot. If you've used pre-cut templates, they should have a little hole drilled through them where the seams cross each other for you to mark the spot. Pre-cut fabric shapes also often include a little template for just this purpose. What's important is that you can clearly see, on the wrong side of the fabric, exactly where each seam should start and finish.

Place your first two pieces, right sides together, and sew your quarter-inch seam from dot to dot, or seam intersection to seam intersection, or up to your pin. If you're working on a sewing machine, take a tiny backstitch at each end of the seam to keep it from coming open. If you're hand sewing, that's not a problem since you have a knot on the beginning end. Loosely knot off the other end at the seam.

Some people recommend marking the dot at the end of the seam with a pin. You pin the two pieces, with the end of the pin coming up in the exact middle of your dot or seam intersection. What you'll do then is *sew right up to but not over* the pin. Pull the pin out and move it to the end dot on your next seam, and repeat.

Now you're ready to tackle the second part of the Y. Again you'll be working from dot to dot and never into the seam allowance or crossing your own stitching. Swivel your fabrics to line up the rough edges for the next seam. You may need to pull some of the fabric that's underneath out to the side to avoid accidently stitching through it, depending on the shape of your block. You should have just your pieces to be joined without any bits stuck in between. Beginning at the very end of the seam you just finished, sew your quarter-inch seam out to the dot (pin) on the open end, that is, from the join outwards.

Finally, you'll do the same for the third branch of the Y. Swivel, start at the join, and sew outwards, stopping when you get to the seam allowance. It looks like this:

1st seam is 1 to 2

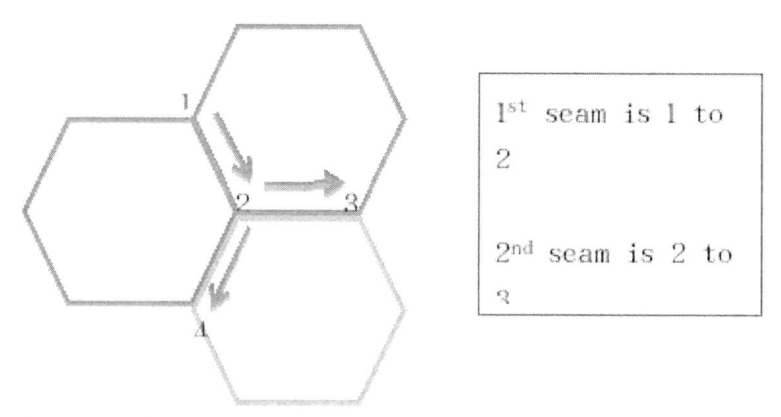

2nd seam is 2 to 3

Don't make a continuous seam from 1 to 3 --- you need the strength of the knots/backstitches to help reinforce the join. If you inadvertently sew into the seam allowance, you'll need to remove the extra stitch(es) or it won't lie flat and will tend to pucker along the seam. Image from Flicker by Gary

Finishing the Quilt Top

If you're working several quilt blocks for your project, you'll connect them to each other in the same manner. You may choose to put some long fabric strips, usually plain colored to match the backing, between your blocks. This is called sashing and is often done around quilt blocks to set them off and help the pieced design to stand out. It can also help to make the finished project larger without doing a lot more pieced blocks. Borders are the same idea, long pieces of fabric, which are added around the outside of the whole quilt top. Borders are also often plain colored fabric, but they can be pieced with the fabric scraps left from making the quilt for a fancy touch. In addition, both borders and sashing, if they are solid colored, provide great areas for some intricate quilting later.

Adding a pieced border to a quilt top. Image from Flicker by Fewer34

You'll attach the sashing and/or border the same way you pieced your block: right sides together, stitch, and press. You'll need to match up the seams on all connecting pieces so your quilt top looks good, and it's not uncommon for them to be slightly off, especially if you have triangle points. Pressing the seams open butterfly-style can make it easier to see to get your seam lines straight. Even if you've used left or right pressing, match the seams, pin them, and sew the cross seam. There will probably be a few that aren't exact, so learn to embrace the imperfection! Native American artisans often intentionally add a 'mistake' to their work if it doesn't already have one --- a different stitch here, a wrong-colored bead or thread there --- to remind them that only the gods are perfect!

Chapter 7: Making Your Quilt Sandwich

Once your quilt top is pieced, pressed, and perhaps sashed, you need to prepare your backing and batting so you can make your quilt sandwich. Hopefully you've bought your backing fabric already. Although the backing can be patch worked, striped, or anything else you'd like, especially for a reversible look, it has traditionally been one plain or printed piece of fabric. Yes, by all means feel free to use a print. That's particularly cute on a crib quilt but completely unnecessary on a pillow or sham, for instance. Whatever you choose, you'll need to cut your backing fabric between four to six inches bigger than your quilt top all the way around, both longer and wider. This gives you two or three inches all around to accommodate stretching, shifting, or whatever else happens by the time you're finished the quilting stage. It's a little insurance.

Batting

Next you need to choose and buy your batting. Batting, if you remember, is the padding layer between your quilt top and your backing material. It not only offers warmth but also serves to give you quilt dimension. Many an antique pioneer quilt had an old wool blanket as batting, but you have many more options today. Batting comes in many different thicknesses, and can be a natural material or synthetic. Some will keep a quilt flatter and easier to cuddle up in; others will make it soft and puffy. In part, your choice will depend on the function of your project, but the method you choose for quilting it will also come into play.

Both polyester and wool battings are shrink resistant. Cotton batting can shrink up to about 5%, giving your finished quilt that puckered antique look we talked about with the pre-washing debate. Cotton batting also makes a quilt that's cooler in the summer because it breathes, while polyester batting doesn't. The cotton-polyester mix is a good compromise. If you're using dark fabrics in particular, stay away from polyester batting unless it has some sort of bonding. The little fibers will work their way up through the fabric over time and stick out (called bearding), and it's incredibly frustrating to live with.

Both hand and machine quilting is best with thin to medium height batting. Cotton, cotton-poly blends, and wool are generally preferred. Thick, or high-loft batting, is good if you'll be tying your quilt rather than stitching. Cotton batting can be a little too dense for beginning quilters to stitch by hand or machine, so the cotton-polyester mix is a better place to start. You'll also see other options, such as silk and flannel, but save those for future endeavors. Fleece fabric is growing in popularity as a batting, or batting/backing combo, because it's lightweight and warm yet thin and soft.

Consider the nature of your project as well. A crib quilt will need frequent washing and drying, while a pillow or wall hanging will not. High-loft batting would make a great comforter but an awkward potholder or placemat. Will your finished project need to drape, or does it need to be a little stiff?

You can buy batting by the yard or in pre-cut sizes, especially for bedding pieces. It should be the size of your backing fabric and it can be pieced. Whatever you choose, check the instructions to see how close the quilting stitches should be. This can vary widely from one manufacturer to another, even within the same type of batting. If your batting has been folded in any way, get it out and lay it flat the night before, fluffing it gently just a little. This will give any crease lines a chance to relax before you put together your sandwich.

Layering and Basting

Your main challenge here will be to keep your layers flat and stationary without wrinkling. The floor is a good place to work on this, or on a large table for a smaller piece. Lay your backing out wrong side up. You want the right side of the backing to be on the outside of the sandwich! Smooth it flat, and you may want to use some painter's tape to stick it to the floor or table. Without pulling or twisting it, you want to lay your batting on top of the backing. Get it straight, but handle it gently. Lastly, center your pressed quilt top on the batting and backing, right side up. This puts the right side of your top and the right side of your backing turned out, with the wrong sides of each in contact with the batting.

You'll stabilize your sandwich by basting (large temporary stitching) the layers together so that they don't shift while you're finishing it off. If you plan to hand quilt, you'll baste with a big needle and strong thread in a color that's easy to see against your quilt. If you'll be machine quilting or tying, you can also do this with large nonrusting safety pins if you like. Starting in the center of your quilt, baste outwards through all three layers to a corner. Repeat from the center to the other corners, ending up with a big X on your quilt. Then baste in rows, both vertically and horizontally, about an inch (or two on a large piece) apart. Once everything is secured together, you can remove the tape (if you used it) and get ready to do either quilting stitches or to tie off your quilt.

Chapter 8: Tying and Quilting

Although tying is the least popular option with most modern quilters, it's also the simplest technique for permanently stabilizing the layers, and therefore can be great for beginners, especially if you don't like sewing. I like it for crib quilts using square blocks, and my grandmother used it for any simple utilitarian quilts that didn't have fancy pieced designs, although she called it tufting or tacking. All you're going to do to 'tie a quilt' is to take single stitches through the all the layers, evenly spaced across the quilt. This leaves loose stitch ends on the quilt top or bottom, which you'll then tie into knots.

Tying a Quilt

You need to use a heavier weight thread for this, such as pearl cotton or embroidery floss, or even a lightweight yarn. You'll also need a heavy-duty needle such as a sharp-tipped tapestry needle. Then you need to decide which side you want your knots to be on. It's completely up to you. If you don't want them to show, or if you want to decorate the back of the quilt a bit, then put your knots on the back. To enhance your quilt top, put them on top. You can further decorate by stringing a button on some of the ties. The tails from the knots will fray together a bit when the quilt's washed for a vintage looking 'tuft', particularly when using either yarn and embroidery thread.

Start in the center of the quilt and take a small stitch down through all three layers and back up again, a stitch maybe a quarter to a third of an inch long, leaving a two-inch tail on both ends of the stitch. Make sure you've gone completely through the backing fabric, leaving that small stitch behind. You'll knot these tails with a square knot or a surgeon's knot (one extra wrap over). If you space your ties about four inches apart, you won't have to cut your thread before making the next stitch. You can let it drape loosely over the quilt top in between stitches; then you go back and cut that trailing piece in the middle after you've made a number of stitches. Sewing several stitches at once then tying them all off is more efficient. Be warned, however, that the actual tying of the knots can be hard on your hands, especially on a large project!

Quilting Lines

Whether you are hand or machine quilting, you need to decide on the stitch pattern that you're going to use. The simplest, of course, is to simply make straight lines, either horizontal-vertical or diagonal-diagonal, crisscrossing the entire quilt top. More traditionally, you can quilt about a quarter to a half-inch from each sewing line. If you have plain blocks, sashing or borders, those areas were traditionally quilted in patterns of varying degrees of intricacy. This was completely true of whole cloth quilts before the popularity of pieced blocks. Complex scenes were quilted into the fabric. They're amazing … and somewhat intimidating. There are special tools and techniques for marking quilting designs onto your fabric, but I won't go into those here. Certainly, marking and quilting a beautiful pattern is something to aim for, but for beginners either straight lines or outlining the pieces (stitching in the ditch) is recommended.

Whichever you choose, you're going to need to practice before starting on your quilt top. Getting nice straight lines with tiny quilting stitches is a little harder than it sounds. So, take some scrap fabric and make a small quilt sandwich. You'll need to pick up some quilting thread if you're working by hand. It's a little heavier and less likely to break than the thread used for regular sewing. Knot your thread and then pull it through the top fabric layer. Give a short quick tug and pop the knot through the fabric and into the batting layer, and then bring your needle back to the top. Practice taking small even stitches going straight down and straight up through your sandwich. This is unlike regular hand sewing and more like embroidery or tapestry. Check the back because your stitches should be the same size on both sides of the quilt. With a little practice, you'll get the hang of it.

Hand Quilting with a Hoop

The same is true if you're using a sewing machine. You'll need what's called a walking foot, which moves up and down rather than sliding over the fabric like a normal presser foot. It keeps things from bunching up. Consult you machine's manual for any guidance they have on using it to quilt and check out their information online. Then practice until you're somewhat proficient before starting to quilt your project. When you get started, go slowly and follow your lines.

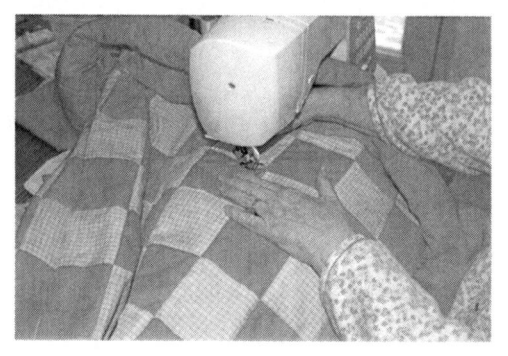

Quilting with a Sewing Machine. Image from Flicker by Jimson

You can mark your quilting lines with washable fabric markers, but if you're doing straight lines there's a quicker way. Painter's tape makes a great straight line to sew along and it comes in several widths. You will sew along the sides of the tape, not through it. You can place the tape so you'll stitch along just one edge or both. It removes easily and it doesn't gunk up your fabric, unless you leave it on for quite a while. It also works for either hand or machine quilting.

You can also become quite a free spirit with your quilting. Circles, swirls, wavy lines, outlines of ducks … whatever you want and wherever you want. Remember that the function of the quilting step is to keep your batting from ending up all bunched in one corner. Anything more than that is up to you. Whether by hand or machine, you can use freeform quilting to express yourself artistically.

If you find that you love the quilting process, consider using more plain blocks and sashing on your next project. This will give you the space to do more creative and more intricate quilting. There are many patterns available and several methods for transferring those patterns onto a quilt top. Plain blocks can also be embroidered or appliquéd. Pieced blocks can be alternated with un-pieced blocks of large figures cut from prints. Quilters are always looking towards their next project!

Chapter 9: Binding Your Edges

Your final step is to bind off, or cover, the edges of your quilt sandwich. There are several different approaches to this, but for anything without curved edges you'll use double-fold straight grain binding. Bias binding is needed to stretch around curves without puckering up. Most quilt patterns tell you how to cut the binding for your quilt, as well as how many pieces you'll need. However, some don't … and some of you are working off the grid from your own pattern. Let's have a short math lesson in calculating binding.

Making binding

A strip of fabric 2 ½ inches wide will give you the standard ½ inch binding used on most quilts. You'll need enough strips to go all the way around the outside edge of your quilt plus 12 inches. First measure the length of your piece; then measure the width. Be exact with partial inches. Add the width and the length together and multiply by two. Now add 12. That number is the total number of inches of binding that you'll need. Don't convert it to feet or yards. Fabric is measured in inches, so stick with that to avoid confusion. To figure out how many strips of fabric you'll need to cut, take that big number you just came up with and divide by 40, which is the usable wide of most purchased fabric. So, how much fabric do you need to have to cut those strips? A quarter of a yard will give you 115 inches of binding; a half a yard yields about 255 inches; and three-quarters of a yard will be about 400 inches.

Let's walk through this for a crib quilt that measures 40 X 50 inches. First we add the length and the width (40 + 50) to get 90 inches. Multiplied by two, it's 180 inches. Add on 12 inches (for corners and piecing the strips together) and we need 192 inches of binding for our crib quilt. Using a standard width fabric, which will give us about 40 inches with the selvage edges cut off, we divide 192 by 40. That comes out to 4.8, rounded up to 5 strips of fabric to cut. If our strips will be 2.5 inches wide, we multiply 5 strips by 2.5 inches to get 12.5 inches, a little over a third of a yard. So we need a third of a yard minimum to cut our binding strips. Personally, I don't like to play things too close and maybe run short, so I'd get about a half yard. If I don't make a cutting error and I haven't made a math error, I'll have some extra that I can use for piecing in my next quilt.

To cut the binding strips, first lay your fabric out flat (pre-washed and ironed if you did that for the rest of your quilt). Next, measure your 2.5 inches across, mark and cut. You need to remove the selvage, the very tightly woven strips that run up each outer edge of the fabric. Cut them off clean and straight. Repeat until you have the number of strips that you'll need.

Now you need to sew the strips together, by hand or machine. The connecting seams can't be straight, that is you can't just seam the end of one strip to the end of the next. That would give you a stack of seam allowances all in one spot, creating a big bump. They need to be joined at a 45-degree angle. To do this, place the end of one strip on top of another at a right angle (right sides together). You'll be sewing at an angle from the right edge of the overlapped pieces up to the top edge, creating a little triangle on the upper right. Pin this first and try to open out your material. If it doesn't make a straight piece, you have the seam running the wrong way. Adjust and check again. Then sew. Trim off this little triangle, leaving a seam allowance next to your stitching. Connect all your strips this way, and check each one before sewing and cutting. It's really easy and very frustrating to end up with a right angle connection.

Press your seam allowances open to keep your binding nice and flat. This helps prevent bumps once you attach it to the quilt. Finally, fold the whole big strip in half lengthwise, with the wrong sides together, and press it. Trim one end of the strip to a 45-degree angle, slanting the same direction as your seams. Fold under a quarter inch on that edge and press. Your binding is good to go!

Finally you need to prepare your quilt sandwich to be bound. It should be quilted or tied by now, and if you haven't already removed the basting or pins, now's the time. Trim off the excess backing and batting, making them even with your quilt top all around. Straighten the corners and sides, if you need to, by cutting off just a little.

Attaching the binding

You attach your binding to the topside of your quilt first. Then it will be folded over the sandwich edge and stitched to the backing. To attach the binding, start in the middle of a side, lining up the raw edges of the binding with the raw edges of your quilt and with the angled end that you trimmed and pressed earlier. Begin sewing about three or four inches from the end of the binding strip, leaving yourself plenty of room to tuck in the other end once you get all the way around. Make a quarter inch seam going through all the layers.

Binding a Quilt by Hand. Image from Flicker by Remy

When you approach the corner, turn the quilt so you'll be headed along the next side. Fold the binding out away from the quilt. You'll see a little triangular fold. Now fold the binding back along the new side even with the raw edge. There will be a little fold of fabric underneath and a nice straight corner. You may want to pin this in place to keep it nice and tidy. Next you'll sew over the fold until you're a quarter inch from the corner; then turn and sew along the new side. Repeat the folding process at each remaining corner.

You'll stop when you're between three or four inches of your starting point. It's time to connect your binding ends. Lay the end over the beginning. You want the pieces to overlap by about an inch or so. Trim the end to the same angle as your beginning piece. Check that carefully because it's nasty to try to repair an error here. You're just going to tuck that end inside the fold of the beginning piece, and again you may want to pin this. Finally, finish stitching the binding to the quilt, going all the way to your first stitches. Take a few small stitches to anchor down the folded edge where the beginning and the end of the binding meet up.

Now it's time to fold the binding over the raw edges of your quilt, enclosing all the layers. Many people pin it all down at this point, while others use binding clips. You can also use small plastic clothespins. Even if you've machine stitched your binding so far, most people sew the rest by hand. This is more like regular hand sewing, but you do want to keep the sewing unobtrusive by using a running tack stitch. First take a little stitch in the backing fabric and pull the thread through. Now you'll run your needle through about a quarter inch of the binding, popping it in and out of the fold. Catch a small bit of the backing and continue. When you come to the corner, fold the binding toward the backing, tack down the fold, and keep going. Once you're all the way around, take a few stitches to secure the ends of the binding together.

You're done!

Chapter 10: Finishing Your Project

If you've chosen a flat project like a placemat or crib quilt, you're completely finished. If you had a pillow or sham in mind, you'll still need to make and attach the back panel. A wall hanging will do best if you attach a quilt sleeve to hang it with (instructions for that are in the next chapter). In any case, you'll want to get all your cutting templates organized inside a bag or envelope, labeled with your pattern name, and tidied away. Save fabric scraps, extra batting, and markers for your next project.

How do you care for your quilted project? Particularly if it's completely hand sewn, your quilt needs gentle care. Mild detergents and the gentle cycle are definitely called for and will help prevent fading. Expect a little shrinkage, especially if you didn't prewash, and some puckering here and there along your seams and quilting lines.

This is the time to do a little reflection on your quilting experience. Think about your favorite part and your least favorite part. Very few quilters love every part of the process, as I told you in the beginning! Was designing your favorite activity, playing with color, print, and shape? Or did you love the precision of cutting? Was it piecing, or stitching the quilt lines? Let these be your guide for choosing and designing your next project. You can challenge yourself with a new tool, new shapes, or more intricate quilting the next time around.

There's the whole world of pre-cut shapes to explore and the joys of the jellyroll.

If you can dream it, you can quilt it! You've just gotten your feet wet as far as quilting, so jump on into the pool. In the next chapters I'll show you some other types of quilts and quilting that you may want to try.

Chapter 11: Project 1- Modern Placemat Walk-Through

This placemat uses offset strips of different colors and sizes to create a striking modern look, but the construction is very simple. Each finished placemat will measure 12 X 18 inches. If you sew, you probably already have some fabric scraps that you can use for the stripes. Otherwise you only need small pieces in 8 prints or colors plus a neutral solid. Your pattern will look like this:

This pattern is best balanced if you do the first and last short stripe [the end ones] on each placemat in the same fabric. Image from Flicker by Gardo

Your small squares on the front can be the same as your backing and binding, so plan on a yard of a solid color that coordinates with or accents your prints. The other option is to buy extra of your prints to use as backing. You could use the same print for the backing on each placemat or a different one for each. You could even use solid colors for your strips in a gradient or a rainbow arrangement. The final look is totally up to you! The total amount of material you need to purchase will depend on how many placemats you want to make. Multiply it out for sets of four, six, or eight. You'll also need a 14 X

20-inch piece of batting for each placemat. Polyester or a cotton-poly blend works well for placemats, especially in a low loft. It stands up well to machine washing and drying, and it doesn't shrink like all-cotton does. It's also easy to quilt, particularly if you're doing it by hand.

Be creative with your choices of prints or colors for this. Hold the pieces next to each other and see how they look. Your fabrics do not need to be all the same colors or scale, so try to put some sharp contrast and variety in there. Do make sure that all eight look good together since you'll have a one stripe of each on each placemat! Your neutral color should probably be a solid so it highlights your prints, but don't limit yourself to off-white. Any solid color will do, even black, so choose something that you like and that blends with all your prints. You could even use a very muted pale print, or a bright one if you're using solid colored stripes.

Placemats will be washed and dried many times, so make sure to prewash your fabrics. Once dried, iron them nice and smooth, and I'd recommend using a little starch or spray sizing to make them a bit easier to work with. Then you'll be ready to cut. You won't need to make templates for this project since you can cut your strips with just a ruler.

For each placemat you'll need to cut 5 strips that are 2.5 X 8.5 inches --- two from the same print and the other three each a different print. You're using four prints here, cutting two strips that match. From your other four prints, cut a strip from each that is 2.5 X 9.5 inches. You'll want to do all your cutting at once, so double this for two placemats, quadruple for four, etc. Each set of nine strips will have two short strips that match, but those will be different for each placemat.

Next cut the small end pieces that you'll be adding to your stripes. Cut some 2.5-inch long strips since they're all that size, then cut your smaller pieces from that. For each placemat you want ten 2.5-inch squares and 8 2 X 2.5-inch pieces. Again, cut enough for however many placemats you'd like. You can also cut your 14 X 20-inch backing piece so it's ready to go.

Arranging your prints is your next step. Put two matching strips on the outer ends and arrange (and rearrange) the pieces in between, alternating long and short, until you like the look of it. If you're making more than one placemat, plan out each one at this time. Stack your arranged strips in your chosen order and either pin them together or set the stack aside where it won't be disturbed.

Now you'll be assembling your pieces. Machine sewing will be sturdier, but you can hand-sew if you like. Using a quarter-inch seam, with right sides together, attach a 2.5-inch square to both short ends of each 8.5-inch long strip. Then connect the 2 X 2.5-inch pieces to both short ends of the longer strips. When you've completed your stripes with the neutral on both ends and the print in the middle, heat up your iron.

Remember you'll press each seam twice. First put it on the board just as you sewed it and press to set the stitching. Then open it up and press your seam allowances to one side. Next you'll sew the stripes together in the order you decided upon earlier, starting at one end and working to the other. Don't forget to press each seam as you go along. Once your top is assembled, trim the edges nice and straight (if you need to), using a ruler.

It's time to make your quilt sandwich, so lay out your backing with the right side down. Place your batting on top. Your pieced top is smaller, so center it on your sandwich. Remember that the right side needs to be up, facing you. Double-check that the backing and the top both have their wrong sides next to the batting. You can use long basting stitches to hold your sandwich together, but on something this size it's easier to use large safety pins. Start in the middle, working your way outwards, and try to place your pins or stitches away from your seams. That will make it easier to quilt around them instead of having to move them.

The best quilting pattern for this placemat is also the easiest. Keeping the quilting lines parallel to your seams will enhance the vertical-striped motif. Use a straightedge ruler and a washable fabric pen; lightly mark a line a quarter-inch from both sides of each seam. You'll again start in the middle and work outwards. This helps to keep your piece smooth and avoids getting a lumpy spot anywhere. Using small up-and-down quilting stitches, follow your quilting line up one side of your center stripe. Check to make sure you're going cleanly all the way through. You need to try to keep your stitches on the bottom the same size as your stitches on the top. If you're machine quilting, use a small stitch length and go slowly so your lines are very straight. Next you'll do the other side of your center stripe. Alternate sides as you work away from your center stripe, quilting along each side of each seam in order. You don't need to quilt the raw edge because the binding will take care of that. Once you have finished your quilting, you'll again even up your edges using a ruler and scissors to trim each side. Cut away the extra batting and backing to make them even with your top.

You have two options when it comes to binding off your placemat. You can make the binding, or you can use purchased bias tape binding in a two-inch width. Pre-made binding is by far the most popular option for small projects like this. It's already seamed and folded, so you'll just need to sew it on. If you can use a solid color, give it a try because it will save you a lot of work. You can match or contrast with your top or backing. However, if you want to use this project as a learning experience, cut two strips 2 X 42 inches long to make your binding. Refer back to Chapter Nine for detailed instructions on how to make and attach your binding.

That's one placemat finished! Make as many more as you need, and enjoy sprucing up your table with something that expresses your personality and tastes exactly. These placemats also make a very nice gift, and they can be customized for different holidays, occasions, or people by your choices with the colors and prints. A special birthday placemat is a lot of fun, particularly for children, and placemats for under a pet's dishes are becoming very popular as well.

Chapter 12: Project 2- T-Shirt Quilt Walk-Through

Using old t-shirts to make a quilt is a lot of fun. It's also a great beginners project! Who doesn't have t-shirts that they don't want to throw away because those shirts are great memories from vacations, rock concerts, sports or other events. T-shirt quilts make fantastic gifts, and you can even use old ones that are torn, stained, or outgrown. Keep the graphics and the memories, but clear the shirt out of the drawer. It's also easy to augment your own supply from friends, thrift shops, and garage sales. Your T-shirt quilt can be any size you like from a throw for the couch to a bed-sized quilt. You can fill out the space for the size you want by adding sashing, borders, or by alternating your T-shirt blocks with other fabric blocks.

Collect all the t-shirts you're thinking to use. Don't overlook those smaller logos, slogans, or designs on the backs, pockets, and sleeves that you might also want. Wash all your t-shirts, and if you are using any that haven't been worn you'll need to wash those at least twice to get that stiff sizing out. Using fabric scissors, cut the bits you want out of each t-shirt, leaving lots of extra fabric around each one to allow for sewing. You'll be adjusting the sizes later. Now sort your images by size.

Decide what size your blocks are going to be, based on your largest design. Many t-shirt quilts use very large blocks, such as 15-inches square, so don't let the size of some of those graphics scare you. Your medium and smaller pieces can be grouped to fit into the larger-sized block. You can piece medium pieces as the center of a quilt block, filling out the space with regular quilt fabric, perhaps in a solid color to highlight the graphics. Use the smaller logos alternated with regular fabric as well. You can add borders around a t-shirt piece to bring it up to block size. Once you know the size of your quilt block, you can start planning your layout and deciding how much other fabric you'll need.

Apart from whatever fabric you'll need for piecing, sashing, or adding borders, there are a few other things you'll need. The first is called interfacing and it's used to stabilize fabrics. T-shirts are way too stretchy to try to quilt, so you'll need fusible woven interfacing for this project. Don't get an interfacing made for knits! Your goal is to make your t-shirt fabric non-stretchy. Some fusible interfacing needs to be washed before you use it so follow the instructions that the manufacturer provides.

You're also going to need fabric for your backing. This can be normal cotton fabric, but flannel and fleece are really fun. If you use fleece, you won't need batting to make a thin quilt! It can serve as both backing and batting. Otherwise, you need to get batting, and again you can use high-loft if you plan to tie off the quilt but low or medium for quilting.

Now it's time to get your t-shirt bits ready to use. Cut a piece of interfacing about two inches larger than your t-shirt piece. Then follow the manufacturer's instructions on how to fuse it to the back of your t-shirt piece. I wish I could walk you through that, but each brand is a little different. Read their instructions, OK? You may want to try a practice round with your discarded chunks of t-shirt to make sure that you understand what you're doing.

Once that's done, you'll cut each t-shirt piece into the size you'll need it to be, leaving a half inch all around it for seams. Cut your other fabric pieces allowing for half-inch seams as well. You can use a template or not, whatever you feel comfortable with. Sew together any blocks that need to be pieced first, then assemble your blocks as you would for any other quilt top, adding in your sashing (if you're using it) as you go, and finally your borders (if you're using them).

At this point you have two options. You can make your quilt sandwich, with or without batting, then quilt and bind as usual. However, if you hate binding and want to try something new, there is another choice that I'll introduce here. Sometimes it's called the 'reverse-bag method', but many refer to it as 'birthing the quilt'. This is really good if you're going to tie your quilt. If you plan to quilt-stitch it, even simply, you may have a little trouble getting it to lie flat.

To 'birth the quilt', you put your quilt sandwich together differently, so read carefully. First you start with the top of the quilt and put it *right side up*. Then place your backing fabric *right side down* on the quilt top. The two *right sides* of the top and backing are touching in the middle of the sandwich, and the wrong sides are top and bottom. If you're using batting, you'll put it on top of the other two pieces. It's easiest to baste the whole thing to hold it together, but you can use pins. Next you'll sew a half-inch seam around three sides and about two-thirds of the fourth side of your quilt sandwich. This is fast and easy on a sewing machine, but you can hand sew as well. Trim the batting, but not the fabrics, close to the seam. Again, trim ONLY the batting, if you've used it. Then you'll use the small opening that you left to turn the whole quilt right side out. Reach in and push the corners out gently. Remove your basting or pins and then slipstitch the opening closed. Your quilt has been birthed!

Finally you'll tie or quilt it to secure the layers as usual. Some perfectionists might use binding, even on a birthed quilt, but most people don't. The whole idea is really to avoid having to use binding. If you're quilting it, however, you may want to gently tug it in various directions to get it to settle a little flatter around the edges, especially if you've used batting. You may also want to iron it.

Whatever you decide, make sure to quilt from the center outwards so you work any puffiness towards the outer edges.

Chapter 13: Some Special Projects

In this chapter, I'd like to introduce you to some other types of quilting projects that are not traditional pieced work. Both the rag quilt and the puff quilt are great beginners' projects, and work well for machine sewing as well. If you're interested in doing wall hangings, you'll need to know how to make a sleeve so you can hang up your work. For those who love the actual sewing, trapunto is a wonderful variation on normal quilting and can produce some fantastic artistic effects. I'll look at each in turn and provide you with instructions for each project.

Rag Quilts

Rag quilts are put together differently from other pieced quilts. First off, each piece is quilted separately. When they are connected, the edges are left exposed on the top of the quilt. Those edges will fray with washing, producing raggedy lines around each piece. To get those lovely frayed edges, rag quilts use a half-inch seam, which also makes them easier for both beginners and for machine sewing. The back of the quilt has no fraying (just seams) because those edges have all been pushed up to the top. Rag quilts are easy to make and have a casual charm. The only trick is choosing fabrics that will fray nicely. Here's how to do it.

Rag Style Baby Quilt. Image from Flicker by Francis

The best fabrics are all-cotton ones or what are called 'homespun' because they fray very nicely. Flannel is great as well, working up into a very soft quilt. Lightweight denim works well also, but a lot of denim is too heavy. It's hard to sew and makes a very weighty quilt. You'll want your batting to be either completely covered or something that will fray as well, so for a thinner rag quilt you can use flannel as batting as well.

Many rag quilts use simple squares. You can subdivide some of these into two rectangles or triangles to add some visual interest to your quilt, but you'll want your pieces to be on the largish side. It's difficult to work with small pieces. Many people choose squares that start out between eight and ten inches, making the finished size for each square between seven and nine inches. You're leaving a half-inch seam on all sides, if you remember! You'll cut squares of the same size for your backing. The backing on rag quilts is usually done in many different colors and prints, just like the top, but that's up to you. Your finished quilt will be reversible, frays on one side and smooth on the other.

Your batting will need to be cut as well, and it will need to be smaller than your fabric squares. If it sticks out into the exposed seams it will wash away! A 10-inch fabric square will end up being 9-inches after seaming. You'll cut your batting into an 8.5-inch square for this, if you're using traditional cotton, or cotton-poly batting. Flannel batting should be cut in a 9.5-inch square in this case because it can be exposed in the seam and will fray nicely. Once you have your squares cut, you'll assemble your little quilt sandwiches in the same manner that you use for traditional quilted projects.

Put a backing square right side down with your batting centered on top. Place your top square on top of this, right side up. Use a few pins to hold this mini-sandwich together. You'll want to put together a bunch of these little sandwiches, if not all of them. The next step is to secure the layers together.

Most rag quilts use a simple corner-to-corner X to quilt each square, which is one reason they're easy to do on the machine. It's equally simple when hand quilting, and you really don't need to mark your quilting lines unless it makes you feel a little more confident. Like everything in quilting, you can vary this up by doing parallel lines, circles, or whatever you like. It's also fun to change your quilting pattern from square to square, going simple on bright prints, doing lines on stripes, and adding some fancier patterns on the plainer squares. Your pieces do not need to be cookie-cutter copies of each other! You will assemble and quilt each square (or rectangle/triangle if you've gotten adventurous) for your entire quilt. Now you have bags full of quilted sandwiches.

Arranging your quilt can be a lot of fun. Start laying out your squares (or whatever) into rows. The floor works well for this. This process is like assembling a jigsaw puzzle. The arrangement of rows and columns will determine the size and shape of your quilt, and it doesn't have to have right-angled corners. You won't need to put binding around this, so please yourself with size and shape! Try to keep adjoining pieces different and to balance (or group) your lighter and darker squares. Play with light and dark arrangements, as well as with grouping or separating like colors, for different artistic effects. You can get a really nice look by doing a gradient from light to dark (or dark to light) and back again. It all depends on the colors and intensities that you have. Once you've made your final decision, stack your pieces for each horizontal row. I like to label them with sticky notes so I can remember which one comes next.

You'll sew these together by horizontal rows, so take the first two pieces from your first row. Align the *backing sides together* and sew a half-inch seam. Open it out and attach the next piece, again with the backing sides together. It's important to sew with the backs together so that your seams will all end up on top where you want them, and it can be hard to remember if you have sewing experience because traditionally you put the right sides together to work. Once you have the row together, label it. Then do the next row, until all your rows are connected. You don't need to press your seams on a rag quilt.

Next you'll attach each row to the following row, matching your seam intersections. Again make sure the backs are together before sewing so your seams are all on the same side! Also check that you're attaching row 3 to row 2 (and not to row 1). That sounds simple, but it's really easy to get confused. Pin a little label with a 1 on it to the first row to help keep you straight.

Once you have all the rows attached together, you're almost finished. I told you that you don't bind a rag quilt, you just let it fray. You'll need to sew a seam (actually, two is even better) around the entire edge of the quilt a half-inch from the raw edge. If you're machine sewing, take a backstitch on the angle at each corner for strength.

The next step involves a lot of clipping, and you may want to spread it out over a couple of days to spare your hands. What you're going to do is to clip into those exposed seam allowances all over your quilt to encourage it to fray in the wash. You can use any sharp scissors, but you may want to invest in a pair of spring-loaded scissors. They open automatically after each cut and don't have finger holes, which is much easier on your hand. Look for ones that have blunted tips to help you avoid cutting into your stitching. You're going to make cuts about a quarter-inch apart into each seam allowance perpendicular (at a right angle) to the seam line. Don't cut too close to the seam! You'll need to be careful at the corners because you don't want to cut off a chunk of material. Take this process slowly because repairing a cut seam is not something you want to spend time on.

The final step is to wash your quilt and fray those edges. Many people like to use both laundry detergent and fabric softener in the wash, claiming it helps the quilt fray better. You'll have a lot of threads coming loose; so put a filter over your washer drain if you have drainage problems. After washing, check to see if you missed clipping any seams (it's easy to do) and clip them now and rewash. Finally put your quilt in the dryer to remove even more of the loose threads. Check it over for mistakenly cut seams and repair those right away. Most people will wash and dry a rag quilt two or three times to get the fraying just right.

Puff Quilt

A puff quilt, sometimes called a biscuit quilt, is not actually quilted at all. Each square is individually stuffed with fiberfill instead, making tiny little puffy pillows. They're soft comforters that are easy to make, and they're great for baby gifts or lap-sized quilts. These instructions are for a baby-sized (or lap quilt) about 32 X 38 inches when finished. You'll want to plan your color/print arrangement ahead of time on this one, so use some paper to plot it out before getting your supplies. Even a random arrangement using scrap fabrics is easier when charted out ahead of time. Read through all the instructions before starting.

You'll need the following to make a lap-sized puff quilt:

- 3 yards total for the top squares

- 2 yards of muslin (this won't be visible in the finished quilt)

- 1 yard of backing fabric

- 2 packages of double-fold bias tape (for binding)

- thread

- a large bag of fiberfill stuffing

Next you'll need to cut 99 top squares that are 6 X 6 inches, and 99 5 X 5 inch muslin squares. You'll put a top square on a muslin square with the wrong side of the fabric against the muslin. Match the corners and make a little pleat with the extra material in the middle of three of the sides. Pin the pleats to the muslin, leaving the fourth side open. Arrange your pinned squares into rows with all the pleats going the same direction. Using a half-inch seam allowance, sewn the sides to each other along the row, and seam the two end pieces as well. Leave the pins in the unsewn edges! Put each row back into its place as you finish this to keep your layout straight.

Now you're going to sew up the third side of each little pocket. Sew a half-inch seam along the bottom of each row, alternating the direction that the seam allowances are going from row to row. All seam allowances in the first row go to the right; all in the second row go to the left. This will help your rows to fit together more easily later. Remove your pins from the bottom of the row after it's sewn. Again, place each row back in its correct location in your layout as your go along.

Once you have all your rows converted into rows of little pockets, you're going to use the openings in the top of each square to fill it with fiberfill. Plump them up nicely but don't pack them tight --- you'll never be able to sew them if you make them too dense and your quilt will be stiff, not cuddly. Sew a half-inch seam across the open top of each row. Then you'll pin and sew the rows together, puffy sides facing.

Now you are ready to finish your biscuit quilt. Cut your backing fabric to the same size as your quilt top and place it right side down on a flat surface. Put your quilt on top, puff side up, muslin side down. Use safety pins to hold it together. Using a strong thread (embroidery floss is good), you're going to attach the top and bottom pieces together using the tying technique (Chapter Eight). Working from upper right to lower left, tie each corner of each pocket with a square knot. This also helps to keep the stuffing in place. Remove your pins, trim the backing even with the top, and baste around all the outside edges. Apply your bias tape as you would any other binding, starting in the middle of one side.

To make this quilt in other sizes, you can increase the number of squares and rows or you can just make bigger squares. The top squares will be an inch bigger than the muslin squares. This technique can also be interesting done as single squares or blocks of 'biscuits' mixed into a normal patchwork design, creating a high-low effect.

Trapunto

Trapunto is really a technique rather than a project, and it's used to create depth. Certain parts have more batting or stuffing than others, causing them to stick out further on the quilt. People who love doing quilting stitching often like trapunto because it produces a beautiful effect on plain light-colored fabrics and really showcases their stitches. The end result is quite elegant. However, many quilters will use a little trapunto to raise certain figures or shapes on a quilt, particularly combined with appliqué. Either yarn or fiberfill can be used to fill in the space. If you are making pillows or quilts for children, this is definitely something to try. Raising those letters or bunnies is something that most children find delightful!

The first step is to choose your pattern or design. You can get ideas from printed fabrics themselves, from books, from nature, or online. If you're artistic, you can draw your own. Once you've made that decision, you'll need to transfer your design onto the fabric. Use a tool designed specifically for fabric, and always test it on a scrap first. This will do two things for you, helping you to see what color works best and verifying that it will really wash out of your fabric. After you've transferred the design, you have two ways to approach trapunto. Hand sewing and machine sewing use different techniques to get the same result.

When hand sewing, you'll use a muslin backing that's only there to hold the stuffing in place, just as we did when making the puff quilt. Image from Flicker by Jessica

Make sure that your muslin piece is larger than your design, and baste it into place right under your markings. On the right side of your design, you're going to sew along the design lines. Many people use decorative embroidery thread for this, but others prefer something that blends in. Once you've sewn all the lines into the fabric, you're going to turn it over and clip away all but about a quarter inch of the excess muslin from around the edges of your design.

Choose where you want to start, and carefully cut a very small slit in the muslin backing. You cut only the muslin, not the quilt top, so be super careful here. You're making a tiny space that you're going to push the stuffing through, which is why using bulky yarn is becoming more and more popular. Its shape makes it easier to use and it's less messy than fiberfill. You're going to fill that tiny space until it looks full from the front, so flip it over and check several times. If you overstuff, your design will be distorted and small spaces can fill up rather quickly. Once you're satisfied, you simply use a whipstitch to close up the slit. You'll then repeat the process on another piece of the design. When you're finished, remove any remaining basting stitches. If this is part of a larger piece, you'll join it in as usual. Trapunto plain blocks can alternate very nicely with pieced blocks for a quilt top.

When machine sewing, the process is a little different. You won't need any muslin backing. You'll baste the batting onto the back of your transferred design. Then you'll machine stitch along all the lines in your pattern. Instead of trimming away excess muslin, you'll be trimming away the excess batting, leaving it only under the places you want to stay puffy.

Either way you do it, your trapunto piece will then go over regular batting and backing, and your quilt will be assembled as usual. Trapunto simply adds another layer or two of batting. Often the area around the trapunto design is densely quilted but as with so much in quilting, that's a personal choice.

Trapunto can also be used to create tapestry-like scenes, particularly for wall hangings. Many times fine materials, such as silks, velvets, and metallic thread, are used to add effects, and the areas can be stuffed to differing heights. This gives a somewhat 3-D feeling to the design and certainly a lot of texture. If you are of an artistic inclination, look at some of these online. You may get inspired to create your own!

Hanging Sleeves

Whether you make a trapunto wall mural, just want to display a quilt block, or you have a whole quilt to display, hanging sleeves are the way to do it. A hanging sleeve is a simply tube of fabric you sew onto the back of your piece. A dowel or decorative curtain rod can then be slipped through the tube and your piece easily hung. You can buy sleeves premade, but they're fairly easy to make on your own. They can either blend or contrast with your piece.

First measure the top edge of your piece. Cut a 9-inch wide strip of prewashed fabric 2 inches longer than the top edge. Then, fold under 1.5 inches on both ends of this fabric strip, and sew a quarter-inch away from the raw edges. Now you'll fold the fabric strip in half lengthwise with its wrong side inside and pin it. You'll use a quarter-inch seam to sew together the long sides. Press the seam open, one piece to each side, and center the seam in the middle of the sleeve. This seam side will be flat against your hanging piece when attached.

You'll attach this sleeve to the upper edge of your hanging piece by slipstitching the top edge. Scoot the bottom edge up a bit before sewing, so that you leave room in the tube for a dowel or decorative curtain rod. If you attach the sleeve flat, your quilted hanging will bulge out at top to accommodate the support rod. Your support rod should be about two inches longer than your hanging piece, with an inch sticking out of the sleeve at either end.

Very small pieces, such as a single quilt block, won't need a whole sleeve. You can make little triangular top corner pockets from squares of material. The dowel will slide into both pockets and can be supported from the middle for display. Pieces entered in shows will need to have sleeves, but each show sets its own requirements for these.

Chapter14: Two Alternative Piecing Methods

So far I've talked about basic piecing, which used to be called patch working. That's why this style of quilt was, and sometimes still is, referred to as a patchwork quilt. There are, however, two other methods for assembling a quilt block, and both are having a resurgence of popularity right now, although they are very old techniques. One is tremendously well suited for hand sewing; the other is more often done on a sewing machine. Both of these methods can enable a quilter to successfully use shapes that might be difficult and complicated to pull off using traditional piecing. Curiously, they both involve using paper, which sometimes leads to people getting them confused. Each not only has a rapidly growing group of fans but also certain unique advantages.

English Paper Piecing

English paper piecing was immensely popular in the late 1700s, especially in England, which is how it got its name. Now shortened to EPP on most quilting sites, English paper piecing can give a novice quilter the ability to make those acute angles on diamonds and triangles easily and exactly, although the most popular shape by far is the hexagon. All those little 'hexies' that make up the Grandmother's Flower Garden (picture in Chapter Three) can be hand sewn separately and then whip stitched together later. Apple cores, trapezoids, tumblers, clamshells, octagons, and pentagons are also tricky shapes made easier by English paper piecing.

The greatest advantage to EPP is that it's supremely portable. Each piece in a block is hand sewn separately and set aside for assembly later. Modern quilters can EPP while commuting, waiting for an appointment, relaxing in the park, or riding in the car. It's 'lap work'. The necessary equipment is small and easy to carry with you anywhere: a needle and thread, fabric pieces, paper pieces, and a small scissors. It's also a perfect way to use up scrap fabric.

The technique of English paper piecing is simple. Fabric is wrapped over a prepared paper template and basted. The template is usually removed after that piece is sewed to another piece, but sometimes the paper is left in there --- it's up to you. There are some fascinating antique quilts, using paper recycled from newspapers and letters, which still have the paper pieces in place. Because each piece is wrapped to a template, finished sizes are very exact and piecing can be more precise, especially angles. Finished blocks can be pieced together easily, but they are also ready to use as appliqués or converted into trapunto elements on a quilt. English paper piecing puts even an intricate design, like the double wedding ring shown here with its angled wedges, within the reach of the beginner.

When using this method, marking, cutting, and seaming your fabric are not the crucial elements; cutting exact templates is. You can purchase pre-cut paper pieces or make your own from regular paper, blank newsprint paper, cardstock, template plastic, or freezer paper. You'll need to be very accurate with measuring and cutting your patterns, but templates made from cardstock, freezer paper, or template plastic can be reused many times. Whatever you choose to make them from, I'll refer to them as 'paper pieces' in these instructions. A hole punched through the center before you begin to sew will enable you to pop your templates out later fairly easily.

Once you have your collection of paper pieces ready, cut your fabric allowing for at least a quarter-inch on all sides for seams. You should have quite a lot of paper pieces and cut fabric pieces before you begin sewing. These are easily stashed in a plastic bag, along with needle, thread, and small scissors, to be carried with you if you so choose.

To sew your pieces, first center your paper piece on the wrong side of the fabric piece and secure it. You can use a straight pin, a plastic-coated paper clip, or a little daub of glue from an acid-free glue stick to do this. Now you're going to baste your fabric around the paper piece. There are two ways to do this, depending upon your template material and whether you want to have to remove the basting later.

If you've used regular paper or blank newsprint (available with the moving supplies in many places), you can simply baste your fabric to the paper. You'll need to use a basting thread that contrasts with your fabric so you can see it easily for later removal. Fold the fabric over the edge of your paper piece and take small stitches through both paper and fabric inside the quarter-inch seam allowance. Make sharp points at the corners, and continue all the way around the piece. On some shapes, like diamonds, you may need to leave some seam allowance extended at the points rather than bunch it up. This is a nice easy method to use, and your stitch lines don't need to be super straight as long as you stay inside the seam allowance. You will, however, need to come back later and remove the basting stitches.

The second way to do this will be required if you've used cardboard or plastic for your templates since you can't sew through them. It's a second option if you've used paper. You'll take a small stitch through the fabric to secure two folded edges at the corner. Then, you'll take running stitches along the straight (fabric only) until the next corner, where you'll again take a stitch through the folded edges. Using this method, all of your basting stays on the back of the fabric piece so you won't need to remove it later.

Once you have a bunch of basted pieces, you can begin assembling them. Take two pieces and put the right sides together. You'll sew them together by using a small whipstitch, catching just the edge of each piece of fabric with your needle. Don't sew through the paper, just the folded edges of the fabric. If you have any extended seam allowance, from a diamond for instance, make sure to assemble with the extended piece on the back, not poking out on the right side. Once a shape is fully surrounded and attached to other pieces, you can remove the paper/template from it along with the basting stitches.

Once the block is all connected, you may want to 'set' it with an iron and a little light spray starch. It's now ready to use as an appliqué or to connect to other finished blocks.

Foundation Piecing

This second piecing method involves stitching fabric pieces onto a foundation piece that has a pattern printed on it. The foundation can be a light fabric such as muslin, but it is often paper. It's called modern paper piecing, or just paper piecing, in many references and web sites, and therefore it can be easily confused with English paper piecing, even though the process is completely different. Foundation piecing is wonderfully well suited for machine sewing, and it can create those acute angles that are hard to achieve with regular piecing, especially for a beginner.

Below you see a foundation-piecing pattern for a heart block. It looks sort of like a paint-by-number canvas, and that's because paper piecing works in very much the same way. In order for your finished blocks to fit together, you'll need to make multiple copies of the pattern. The traditional way to do this is to trace the pattern as many times as needed. You could try using a photocopier, but they all distort a little bit, especially if you make several copies at a time. The easiest way to get multiple copies without hand tracing is to use the needle punching method. Use your unthreaded sewing machine needle to trace around the pattern, going through several pieces of paper at a time. You can just follow your first set of lines along to make a second batch until you have enough. Then cut pieces of fabric large enough to cover each number on your pattern with some spare fabric left over for the seams. This can be rough cutting; your pieces don't need to be exact (you'll trim them later) but do be sure to leave a seam allowance.

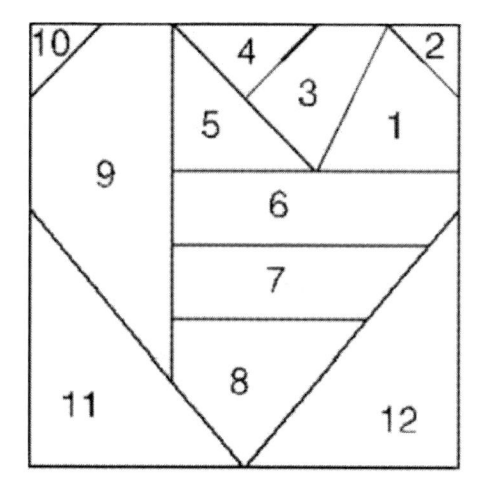

You're going to put your fabric on the 'wrong' side of your foundation pattern, that is, the unprinted side. You'll be sewing on the 'right' side of the paper, through the paper and the fabric. So, put the fabric for piece 1 right side up on the back of the pattern. Image from Flicker by Jason

Hold it up to the light to make sure the fabric is placed to completely cover space 1. You'll probably want to pin it in place or use a little glue stick to hold it steady. Now do the same for piece 2 with the *right side of fabric 2 facing the right side of fabric 1*. Make sure that the two pieces overlap at least a quarter of an inch and that all of area 2 on the pattern is covered with extra fabric for the seam allowance.

Now carefully turn it all over. You'll sew on the line of the pattern that divides piece 1 and piece 2. Do a quick check that you've gotten fabric 2 correctly placed by holding your pattern up to a light source. Fabric 2 should cover the entire area of piece 2 on the pattern with at least a quarter-inch extending over the lines for seams. If it's not correct, you'll need to pick the stitching out, reposition the fabric, and sew it again.

Once you're sure that fabric piece 2 has been correctly positioned and sewn, you're going to trim the seam you've just made. Fold the foundation paper on the seam line you've just made so that the printed sides of that paper are facing each other. This should expose the seam allowance between fabric piece 1 and fabric piece 2. Trim the seam allowance to a neat quarter of an inch. Either scissors or a rotary cutter can be used for this. With very small pieces, you may need to trim a slightly narrower seam allowance to allow them to lie flat.

After your seam is trimmed, unfold the foundation paper and press fabric 2 into position. While finger pressing will flatten the seam enough to continue, using an iron for this step will give you better results. It not only makes a nice flat seam but will also flatten out the fold in the foundation paper, keeping your pattern true as you progress from piece to piece.

Now you'll repeat the previous steps, putting fabric 3 with its right side facing fabric 2 and covering all of foundation area 3. Make sure you have an overlap for the seam and have enough fabric extending beyond the borders of area 3 for later seams. Always check your fabric placement before and after sewing so you can fix any errors immediately. Otherwise, you'll have to unstitch a whole lot of pieces later to get your block correctly put together. With everything held in place, turn it all over and sew the line of the pattern between piece 2 and piece 3. Fold the foundation paper along the seam and then trim your most recently made seam. Press fabric 3 into position and flatten your foundation paper.

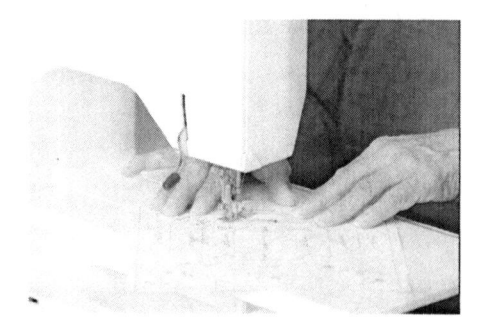

Foundation Paper Piecing. Image from Flicker by Gerald

You'll continue repeating this process for each piece on your foundation pattern, following the numbers and attaching each fabric piece to the one before it. Once all of your fabric pieces have been sewn onto the foundation paper, trim and tidy the edges of the whole block, making sure to leave your quarter-inch seam allowance around all sides of the block. Now, give this all a final pressing and admire your finished quilt block

Your sewing has put little perforations into the paper, so it's pretty easy to tear it off along all those seam lines. Just go gently so you don't break your stitches. You can either remove the foundation paper now, or you can wait until the blocks have been connected to each other before removing it from each block.

Once you try this, I think you'll see that it sounds more complicated to do than it really is. Foundation paper piecing is quick and easy to do on a sewing machine, and there's no precision cutting from templates required. There are many free patterns available on the Internet for you to download and print. Check the pattern instructions carefully, however, for their printing directions because you may need to enlarge the foundation pattern or change your printer settings. Pre-printed foundations can also be purchased at most stores that carry quilting supplies. Like English paper piecing, foundation piecing is an easy way to use of scrap fabric.

Chapter 15: More Common Quilting Terms

As you explore the world of quilting, you'll run across a number of unfamiliar terms. Although I've given you the basics earlier in this book, it's always good to be able to find out what something means, especially as you start exploring quilt blocks and patterns. So here's a longer version of basic quilting terminology.

1. Album quilt: a quilt made with many different quilt blocks, each having a symbolic or sentimental significance. Sometimes a different person makes each block. They may be autographed or signed by the creator of each block, making an Autograph Quilt.

2. Appliqué: small amounts of fabric sewn on top of a background fabric in a decorative design such as curved floral or animal motifs. It's also a great way to cover rips, stains, and other boo-boos.

3. Backing: the bottom or back piece of a quilt.

4. Basting: long stitches used to hold something together temporarily.

5. Batting: the padding layer. It's also called wadding or stuffing.

6. Bearding: fibers wiggling from the batting through the quilt top. They form a fuzzy surface on the quilt and may be caused by static electricity. Bearding is most often associated

with polyester battings and is a particular nuisance on dark fabrics.

7. Betweens: small thin sewing needles used for hand quilting.

8. Bias: the direction running at an angle to the woven fiber direction of a fabric. It's very stretchy.

9. Binding: a strip sewn over the outer raw edges of a quilt

10. Blocks: the basic building piece of a quilt. Most quilts are put together using many blocks of the same pattern

11. Border: pieces of fabric added to a quilt top and framing it.

12. Chain sewing: used in machine sewing, pieces are feed through one right after the other and the connecting threads snipped later.

13. Charm Quilt: a piecework quilt of single squares with no two squares being identical.

14. Cheater's Cloth: fabric printed to look as though it's a pieced quilt top that can then be sandwiched and quilted.

15. Color Wheel: a device used to help evaluate the blending or contrasting qualities of different colors.

16. Directional Print: a fabric where the print runs in a specific direction, like stripes or pictures of candy canes.

17. Fat Eighth: piece of fabric approximately 9 X 18 inches.

18. Fat Quarter: a piece of fabric approximately 18 X 22 inches, also known as an FQ.

19. Finger Pressing: using your fingers to flatten out a seam instead of an iron.

20. Free-Motion Quilting: a way of machine quilting with the feed dogs lowered so the fabric can be freely moved in any direction.

21. Fussy Cut: to cut only a certain figure or design part from a printed fabric, like a large flower, and leave the rest unused.

22. Grain: the lengthwise and crosswise threads of a fabric.

23. Hand quilting: stitching with needle and thread through all three layers of a quilt.

24. Hanging Sleeve: a fabric tube attached to the back of a quilted piece to use in displaying it on a wall.

25. HST: a common abbreviation for 'half square triangle', that is a square cut in half diagonally.

26. Jelly Rolls (etc.): pre-cut pieces of fabric for quilting in various sizes and shapes. Each company uses its own names such as Tonga Dimes, Sushi Rolls, L'il Bits, and Charms.

27. Layout: the arrangement of pieces and pieced blocks in a plan.

28. Muslin: a plain, inexpensive fabric used to hold stuffing in place or other utilitarian tasks.

29. Mitered Corner: the corner of a border folded and joined at a 45-degree angle.

30. Motif: a repeating figure or theme.

31. On Point: a square block turned so its corners are up, down, and side-to-side.

32. Patchwork: an older term for what is now called pieced work.

33. Pin-baste: use pins instead of basting stitches.

34. Quilt top: the top layer of a quilt, usually pieced or appliquéd.

35. Repeat: the length on the fabric before a print starts over.

36. Rotary Cutter: a tool much like a pizza cutter for cutting fabric. It must be used on a special mat.

37. Sashing: strips of fabric sewn between pieced blocks to separate them.

38. Selvage: the outer ends on woven fabric that are more densely woven than the rest and are usually cut off.

39. Sharps: small thin and very sharp needles used for piecing.

40. Stitch in the ditch: quilting next to and following your seam lines and echoing your block pattern.

41. Summer quilt: made with a top and backing but no batting.

42. Template: a shape used as a pattern for tracing.

43. Tied Quilt: knotted strings or ties are used to hold the layers together rather than stitching.

44. Trapunto: a stuffed quilted design

45. Walking foot: a presser foot for sewing machines that moves up and down rather than sliding across the fabric.

46. WOF: a common abbreviation for Width Of Fabric, the distance between the selvages.

Conclusion

Quilting involves many different skills apart from sewing. Some love creating and planning the design, some love the piecing, and others love the actual quilting, but everyone loves the finished product! If you've looked around a store that has quilting supplies, you've seen an awful lot of sometimes baffling equipment. Don't be intimidated! You don't need a lot of fancy stuff to make a quilt. Your great-great-granny certainly didn't have all that, and she made gorgeous quilts … and so can you. So, here's a 'how to get started' manual to get you headed in the right direction. After that, it's your road and your quilt. Take two layers of fabric, stitch them together with padding in between, and the why and how are up to you.

From the author

Thank you for purchasing this book.

I really enjoyed writing it, and I've already had some great feedback from readers who enjoyed the book. I hope you too enjoyed it.

I appreciate that you chose to buy and read my book over some of the others out there. Thank you for putting your confidence in me to help you. If you enjoyed the book and you have a couple of spare minutes now, it would really help me out if you would like to leave me a review (even if it's short) on Amazon. All these reviews really help me spread the world about my books and encourage me to write more books!

Sincerely Yours,

Annie Ramsey

Let me recommend you to read my other popular books:

[101 Chicken Low Carb Recipes: A Healthy Way to Lose Weight Naturally](#)

[Diabetes Diet Plan:Diabetic Diet Guidelines for Curing Diabetes and Lose Weight Naturally: Diabetes Diet Cookbook and Recipes to Prevent Diabetes, Boost Metabolism , Diabetes Treatment, Diabetes Tips](#)

Wedding Planning Guide: A Practical, on a Budget Guide to a Sweet and Affordable Wedding Celebration: Wedding ideas, Wedding tips, Step by Step Wedding Planning

Leptin Diet & Leptin Resistance：Top 50 Leptin Resistant Diet Recipes for Weight Loss

Effectively and Naturally.(leptin diet plan, weight loss programs)

Artisan Bread in Five Minutes a Day: A Complete Guide in Making Easy and Delicious Sourdough Bread (Artisan Bread Recipes, No Knead Artisan Bread)

Liver Cleanse and Detox Diet Guide: Top 30 liver cleanse recipes to remove toxins, lose weight, stay healthy and cleanse liver!(liver cleansing foods, natural liver cleanse)

Adrenal Fatigue Diet: Adrenal Fatigue Treatment with the Hormonal Balance and Top 50 Easy to Do Recipes

Anti-Inflammatory Diet: Complete Guide to Relieving Pain and Healing Inflammation with Top 50 Simple and Delicious Recipes

Nutribullet Recipes: Top 51 Nutribullet Smoothie Recipes for Weight Loss, Beautiful Skin, Anti-Aging

Mediterranean Diet Recipes for Beginners: Top 51 Delicious Mediterranean Recipes for Weight Loss Healthy

Anti-Inflammatory Diet: Complete Guide to Relieving Pain and

WITHDRAWN
No longer the property of the
Boston Public Library.
Sale of this material benefits

HOT LINE

Body Blues

by Laurie Beckelman

Series Consultant
John Livingstone, M.D.

Crestwood House
New York

Maxwell Macmillan Canada
Toronto

Maxwell Macmillan International
New York Oxford Singapore Sydney

For Lloyd,
who helps chase my body blues away

Author's Note:
Many teenagers generously shared their thoughts and experiences with me.
The quotes in this book are based on their stories.

Copyright © 1994 Crestwood House, Macmillan Publishing Company

All rights reserved. No part of this book may be reproduced or transmitted in any form or by any means, electronic or mechanical, including photocopying, recording, or by any information storage and retrieval system, without permission in writing from the Publisher.

Crestwood House
Macmillan Publishing Company
866 Third Avenue, New York, NY 10022

Maxwell Macmillan Canada, Inc.
1200 Eglinton Avenue East, Suite 200
Don Mills, Ontario M3C 3N1

Macmillan Publishing Company is part of the
Maxwell Communication Group of Companies.

First Edition
Design: Lynda Fishbourne, Hemenway Design Associates
Packaging: Prentice Associates Inc.
Photos:
Image Bank: Cover, 4, 22, 35, PhotoEdit: (David Young-Wolff) 7, 10, 31, (Freeman/Grishaber) 17, (Tony Freeman) 12, 20, 25, (Rhoda Sidney) 27, (Robert Brenner) 29, (Richard Hutchings) 39, 40, (Myrleen Ferguson Cate) 43.

Printed in the United States of America
10 9 8 7 6 5 4 3 2 1

Library of Congress Cataloging-in-Publication Data
Beckelman, Laurie.
  Body blues / by Laurie Beckelman.—1st ed.
    p. cm.—(Hot line)
  Includes bibliographical references and index.
  ISBN 0-89686-842-7   0-382-24743-4 (pbk.)
  1. Body image in adolescence—Juvenile literature. 2. Self-acceptance in adolescence—Juvenile literature. [1. Self-perception. 2. Self-acceptance.]
  I. Title. II. Series.
BF724.3.B55B43 1994
155.5—dc20   93-31778

Summary: A discussion of body image and how it affects self-esteem. Provides examples of teens who are unhappy with their appearance and offers suggestions for overcoming a negative body image.

HOT LINE

Body Blues

CONTENTS

Attack of the Inner Critic 5

The Body Blues 8

Your Changing Body 13

So What Is Beauty, Anyway? 18

The Impossible Ideal 23

The Truth About Bodies 26

Ten Steps to Beating the Body Blues 30

A Final Word 44

If You'd Like to Learn More 46

Glossary/Index 48

We all worry about our appearance. And we're right to do so. How we look is the first thing others see about us. We should want to look our best. But sometimes we believe that our best isn't good enough.

Attack of the Inner Critic

You're too fat. Too thin. Too short. Too tall. You're too hairy, too hairless, too busty, too flat. Your thighs are flabby, your stomach is huge, your nose is too long, and your skin's full of zits. Your breath smells. Your teeth aren't white. Your muscles are scrawny. Your rear's like a truck. Your hair is too straight. Too frizzy. Too limp. Too mousy. Too dry. Too oily. Too thick. Too . . .

Aaarghhh! It's an attack of the **inner critic**—that inside-your-head voice that *never* thinks you look good enough. Everyone has an inner critic, and one of its favorite targets is the body. According to **psychologists** Hal and Sidra Stone, the inner critic is with us from childhood. It starts life as a helpful voice. Its job: to protect us by pointing out our faults and mistakes before others can. Then we can correct our ways, please other people, and avoid embarrassment or, worse, rejection.

But too often that helpful voice turns harmful. The inner critic gobbles up criticisms and slimes you with them whenever it can. It can turn a mole into a mountain of ugliness. It can start chanting, "Blob, blob, blob, blob" just because you gained two pounds. It compares you with magazine models and movie stars—unfavorably, of course. It eyes the other kids at school and notes every way in which you are different, then turns each difference into a fault. It remembers your father's teasing and your mother's "helpful" diet advice and the unkind comments of some kid in the third grade. It can turn the negative opinions of others into your truths. But you can stop it.

Your inner critic is only one part of you. You can listen to it. You can even thank it for sharing its thoughts. But you don't have to believe everything it says.

We all worry about our appearance. And we're right to do so. How we look is the first thing others see about us. Sometimes our appearance is the first thing others judge us by. We should want to look our best. But sometimes we believe that our best isn't good enough. We think we have to look a certain way to be liked, accepted, or loved. These beliefs can give us the **body blues.**

When we get the body blues, we let our feelings about our bodies affect our feelings about our entire selves. Too often, we confuse looking good with being good and, by extension, with being lovable and valued. We begin to feel bad not only about our bodies but also about ourselves. During the teen years, when our bodies are changing so much and our need for acceptance is so great, the body blues seem as common as the flu.

This book is about beating the body blues. It is about the normal changes of adolescence and how they can sow the seeds of self-doubt—seeds that may grow into the body blues. It is also about the dangers of trying to mold ourselves to the inner critic's ideal. But most of all, it is about setting realistic goals for beauty and health so that you, not your inner critic, is in control of your body and your life!

The inner critic gobbles up criticisms and slimes you with them whenever it can. It can turn a mole into a mountain of ugliness.

The Body Blues

"Some guy wanted me to go to a pool party," says Diana. "But I had to say no. If he saw my thighs, he'd puke. They're *so* gross!" Diana wears a size 5.

"I look in the mirror and all I see is nose, nose, nose," says Marc. "I can still hear my uncle saying to my dad, 'Poor kid. He's got the family honker.'" Yet Marc's nose, though large, hardly dominates his face. It doesn't hold your attention nearly as long as his soft brown eyes and his smile.

Diana and Marc have the body blues. They ignore what's good about how they look and concentrate on what they think is wrong. People get the body blues for different reasons. Some have a **body image** that does not match reality. For instance, Diana thinks that her thighs are "gross" even though she wears a size 5. She has an inner picture of her body that stays the same no matter how she really looks. Others have an accurate sense of how they look but exaggerate the importance of their differences. Jane has **scoliosis,** a curved spine. She says she'll never let a boy put his arm around her because she is embarrassed to have him touch her back.

Diana, Marc, and Jane have lots of company. More than 30 percent of American teens and adults who answered a *Psychology Today* survey didn't like their overall looks. Even more people were unhappy with their weight. The dissatisfaction was greatest among teens and young adults. Although this survey was done in 1985, more recent studies suggest that people are still just as down on their looks, if not more so.

The problem is most widespread among girls. Our **culture** gives boys and girls different messages about what should make them feel proud of their bodies. For boys the ideal is a strong and athletic body. For girls it is a thin one. Although many girls today value strength and fitness, too, these new aspects of beauty have not replaced the old one. They have added to it.

Studies show that girls are more unhappy with their bodies than boys. They want to look different from the way they do and often see

A government study of more than 11,000 teens across the country found that almost half the girls were trying to lose weight.

losing weight as the key to a better body shape. A government study of more than 11,000 teens across the country found that almost half the girls were trying to lose weight. Most boys thought their weight was okay, although some thought they were too skinny. Other studies have found that as many as 70 percent of all girls want to lose weight, but that only 15 percent are actually overweight.

Why some people get the body blues and others do not is hard to say. Like Marc, they may have heard negative comments about some part of their bodies or faces since childhood. Maybe they've been teased at school. Or perhaps their parents place too much emphasis on weight and looks. Some studies suggest, for example, that when mothers criticize their daughters' weight and appearance, the daughters are more likely to have eating problems.

People who criticize our looks are often "put-down pros" who are insecure about their *own* appearance. Their comments may really have more to do with their fears than with our looks. But we aren't always aware of this. We think something is wrong with us. We get the body blues.

We can also get the body blues simply because we are unsure of ourselves. Since uncertainty about our changing bodies is a normal part of being a teen, we are more likely to get the body blues at this stage of life.

Sometimes the put-down pros make our worries worse. We may develop a poor body image.

Your Changing Body

"**I** was really fat in middle school," says Alex. "And boy, did I get dumped on. Kids started calling me 'Al Licks.' They'd yell things like, 'Hey, Al, been lickin' ice cream again?' Man, I used to get so mad I felt like smothering them in ice cream. Then, in ninth grade, I got real tall. I wasn't fat anymore—just big. I went out for basketball and football and made both teams. *No one* calls me Al Licks anymore."

Adolescence is a time of rapid and dramatic change. Your rate of growth is faster now than at any time except infancy. You may be going through **puberty**. During puberty, girls develop breasts and broader hips. They begin to menstruate. Boys develop larger genitals and are able to ejaculate. Their voices deepen and they grow facial hair. Both sexes grow body hair and gain height and weight. Because of different **sex hormones**, girls usually add more body fat than boys and their hips widen. Both changes are necessary for having babies. Boys add more muscle and bone tissue. Their shoulders, arms, and thighs develop.

Although puberty usually starts around age 10 or 11 for girls and 12 or 13 for boys, it can come earlier or later. The rate at which changes occur differs from teen to teen, too. Some teens have reached their adult height and full sexual maturity by age 14 or 15. Others are not fully developed until age 18 or 19.

These normal differences in the onset and rate of change leave many teens wondering if their bodies are normal. Those who develop very early or very late may worry a great deal. "By the time I was in the seventh grade, all the girls had bras but me," recalls Monica. "I was afraid something was wrong with me, but I couldn't say so. Instead, I pretended I was like everyone else. I'd let the strap of my slip show so kids would think it was a bra. Some days I almost convinced myself."

Some kids who experience puberty earlier or later than their friends may worry that they have done something to damage themselves. They haven't. Bodies develop at different rates for a number of reasons. How we act and what we think are not among them. **Heredity** is. A boy whose father or grandfather was the first in his crowd to shave may develop facial hair early, too. A girl whose mother got her first period at age 15 might be destined to be a late bloomer. By talking with our parents and grandparents about how their bodies changed when they were teens, we can sometimes better understand how ours are developing.

It's normal to worry about our bodies when they are changing so much. Some changes that adolescence may bring, like acne or body odor, are embarrassing. Others can be scary. Girls may find one breast growing faster than the other. Or they may have cramps when they get their periods. Boys may develop some breast tissue or be troubled by wet dreams. Experiences like these are almost always normal. Breasts even out in girls and disappear in boys; wet dreams are a passing phase, and most people outgrow acne. But if some changes in your body bother you, speak to a doctor or an adult you trust. You have a right to have your fears heard.

Sometimes the put-down pros make our worries worse. We may get teased at school. Parents or other adults may laugh at our concerns or add to them with insensitive comments. Monica remembers the day she finally got up enough courage to ask her mother for a bra. "My mother laughed and said, 'For what?' I cried myself to sleep that night. I thought I'd *never* have breasts."

The inner critic laps up these reactions and exaggerates them. We can hear it saying:

> You'll *never* have breasts, so no boys will ever like you.

> You'll always be a peanut. What girl would want to go out with you?

> Your face is so covered with zits that everyone thinks you're ugly. Forget about dating—no one even wants to be your friend.

If the put-down pros and our own inner critic convince us that these things are true, we may develop a poor body image. Body image matters because it is part of our **self-esteem.** Good self-esteem helps us feel happier and accomplish more.

For some teens, the bad feelings that come from a poor body image linger long after the teenagers have left awkwardness behind. "Remember how I said that no one calls me Al Licks now?" asks Alex. "Well, that's not completely true. Sometimes *I* call me Al Licks. I'll be looking in the mirror, and I hear this little voice in my head, 'Al Licks, Al Licks,' and I feel like a tub again. I have to say to myself, 'Hey, Alex. You're *Alex*, remember?' "

People's comments and our own fears can be hard to

> *Body image matters because it is part of our self-esteem. Good self-esteem helps us feel happier and accomplish more.*

forget. But they don't have to rule our body image. Like Alex, we can recognize our fears for what they are: fears, not reality. It also helps to understand why we feel so much pressure to look a certain way.

So What Is Beauty, Anyway?

"I always hated my body," says Margaret, a woman now in her forties. "I've always been big-boned, tall, and heavy. I can't tell you the number of diets I've tried. But two years ago my family had a reunion. Cousins and cousins of cousins came from all over the country.

"I was talking to one of my relatives, thinking how attractive she looked, when I suddenly realized something: She's built just like me! I looked around the room and saw all these people—*my* people—who were built just like me. What an eye-opener! I realized that I have the body I'm supposed to have. And it's not fat—at least not to me. It's strong, healthy, and ample."

Margaret is big, but she is also attractive. She carries herself proudly and smiles with warmth and confidence. Observing her sharp green eyes and thick black hair, some people might even find her beautiful. In earlier times, her body type would have been thought beautiful, too. The seventeenth-century artist Peter Paul Rubens painted well-rounded, fleshy women. They were the ideal of his era. Nearly three centuries later, the French painter Pierre-Auguste Renoir was still celebrating the beauty of soft curves.

To a large degree our culture defines what we consider beautiful. In Rubens's and Renoir's times, the culture saw full-bodied women as beautiful. For a long time Americans prized rounded bodies, too. The ample "Gibson Girl" was the ideal of the early 1900s. But today, thin and trim spell beautiful. Fashion magazines, billboards, ads, TV, and movies all show the same image of beauty. Its skin might be brown, black, or white; its hair might be frizzed, straight, or wavy; but its body is lean and muscled. Our beauty ideal reflects fashion, not the reality of what most women look like.

Of course, thinness is not the only yardstick our culture uses to measure beauty. Other ideal images include high cheekbones, straight noses, large eyes, white teeth—the list could go on and on. But what really makes a face attractive? Is it simply the physical features or is it something else?

Tara and Ricky probably look attractive to others because they feel attractive inside. They realize that how they look does not determine their value as people.

20

"Something else!" says Sherri. "Take my best friend, Tara. Her features aren't great. Her nose has a bump, her lips are real thin, and her hair's this real mousy color. But she's beautiful! And I'm not the only one who thinks so. You should see all the guys who ask her out!"

Raul agrees: "One of the most popular guys in my class has a harelip. You know, he was born with something wrong with his lip. The girls all think he's cute. If it were me, they'd probably find it disgusting! But it doesn't stop Ricky, not one bit!"

Tara and Ricky probably look attractive to others because they feel attractive inside. They realize that physical appearance does not determine their value as people. Through the way they walk, talk, smile, and act, they communicate that they think they're worth being with. And others agree.

Today's body ideal is so thin and toned that few people can meet it. This is most true for females. Female bodies are supposed to have fat.

The Impossible Ideal

But feeling good about your body when it doesn't match the latest fashion can be hard. Today's body ideal is so thin and toned that few people can meet it. This is most true for females.

Female bodies are supposed to have fat. In fact, a girl cannot menstruate and, therefore, bear children, until at least 17 percent of her body weight is made up of fat tissue. During her teens, an average girl goes from about 8 to 20 percent body fat. Yet the body ideal suggests that girls should look more like boys than like women. Research shows that over the past 50 years the standard of female beauty has become thinner and thinner. Models are thinner. Actresses are thinner. Even *Playboy* centerfolds and Miss America contestants are thinner.

The pressure to measure up to this ideal is intense. Almost 1 in every 10 TV ads focuses on beauty. These ads imply that the right hair color, the right deodorant, the right body shape, or the right jeans are the key to love, fun, and happiness. Of course, the advertisers define what is "right." That's how they get us to buy what they're selling!

The message that looking right brings success isn't only in the ads. Think of the romantic leads you've seen in movies or on TV. Are many of them fat? Are many of them less than beautiful? It's no wonder that the inner critic looks at an extra 2 pounds as if it were 20!

Our culture has accepted the media hype. Diet books, diet shakes, and fitness tapes become best-sellers. Supermarket tabloids report the diet triumphs and tragedies of the stars as if they were world events. We can even buy diet foods for pets! Researchers have many ideas about why we are so obsessed with thinness. Some say it is part of our fear of aging. Most people get heavier as they age. By fighting the flab, we deny our own aging, or so the theory goes. Others claim that women have had to act and look like men to make it in the workplace. They say that the stress on thinness often forces women to reject the bodies they were born with.

Still others consider thinness a symbol of self-control in a world that feels frighteningly beyond our control. By controlling our weight, they argue, we reassure ourselves that we can control our lives.

However it came to be, the current beauty ideal can leave us feeling insecure. How can we hope to be as thin

Our culture has accepted the media hype. Diet books, diet shakes, and fitness tapes become best-sellers.

and beautiful as a cover girl? Or as broad-shouldered and thin-hipped as the latest hunk? Most of us can't. Our **genes** determine our basic body shape. While exercise and diet can influence our health and the way we look, they cannot change the basics. If our parents and grandparents are short and burly, chances are we will be, too. If they are big-boned and broad, so, most likely, are we.

What's more, even film stars and models are not as perfect as they look. They have makeup artists to mask pimples and highlight cheekbones and photographers to airbrush out spots that makeup cannot hide. Film stars even have body doubles. The body double's well-formed leg, torso, or back substitutes for the star's lumpy, bumpy, or otherwise imperfect one. Dinosaurs and UFOs aren't the only special effects Hollywood has to offer!

But too often we fall for the image even when we know it is not real. We forget that most people will never match the ideal, no matter what it is. How do you think skinny women felt back in the days when extra fat was seen as attractive? They probably tried to gain weight!

The Truth About Bodies

The next time you're in the school lunchroom, take a look—a really good look—at the people around you. Look at the shape of their bodies and their height and their weight. Look at the length of your classmates' feet and the size of their noses.

The truth is, bodies come in all shapes and sizes. So do facial features like noses. Normal is different for each of us. This holds for weight as much as for height and shape. Our genes affect our weight. How do we know? Consider the case of identical twins. They have identical genes. Even when such twins are separated early in life and raised by different families, their adult weights are close. Their genes **predispose** them to being heavy or thin.

This doesn't mean that what we eat has no effect on our weight and shape. Of course it does. A naturally thin person can overeat and become heavy; a naturally heavy person can diet and become slim.

The truth is, bodies come in all shapes and sizes. Normal is different for each of us. This holds for weight as much as for height and shape.

But as soon as food intake goes back to normal, so does weight. Many experts now believe this happens because each of us has a natural weight, called a **set point.** You can think of the set point as like a thermostat setting. Just as a thermostat keeps a room at a steady temperature, so our bodies keep our weight around the set point.

When we try to whittle our bodies down to cover-girl slimness, we wage war against ourselves. It's a war we are bound to lose. And when we lose, we feel worse than ever. The inner critic starts in: You failed again. You have no self-control. You should be thin. Each comment is a hammer blow, pounding our self-esteem into the ground.

We need to wage a different war—not against ourselves but against the image that enslaves us. To do this, we need to pay more attention to what we like about ourselves and less to the inner critic and the put-down pros.

"I'm a chub, okay? I mean, no one would nominate me for prom queen or anything," says Kaitlin. "And I hated myself for it. I'd look at fashion magazines and feel rotten. Maybe I'd be on a diet, and then I'd look at some model and think, 'I'll never look like that. Who am I trying to fool?' So I'd go pig out on chips to make myself feel better. One day, in the middle of a bag of chips, I suddenly thought, this is crazy! Here I am pigging out because I can't look like Cindy Crawford! But I'm just making myself fatter.

"I'd pig out on chips to make myself feel better. One day I suddenly thought, this is crazy! Here I am pigging out because I can't look like Cindy Crawford!"

"I don't know what clicked, but something did. I was so tired of hating myself." Kaitlin stopped spending so much time looking at magazines. Instead, she started taking after-dinner walks with her kid sister. She also got a great new haircut and some new, flattering clothes. She began riding her bike again. She loved riding but had stopped after a boy on her block said her rear looked like a pancake spread over the seat.

"People started telling me how great I looked. They'd ask if I had lost weight. I didn't even know. And I didn't really care."

Like Kaitlin, you can stop waging war on yourself. The first step is to clarify your goals. Then follow the other steps in this book for a healthier, happier you.

Ten Steps
to Beating the Body Blues

Step 1: Clarify Your Goals

"I believed that being thin would make me happy," writes Sally Tisdale, an author who has struggled with her weight all her life. "I lost weight," she continues, "and wasn't happy."

For Tisdale, happiness, not weight loss, was the real goal. Once she became aware of this, she gave up the struggle with weight for the more important struggle for self-acceptance.

Ask yourself: What do I think would be different if I were thin? If I were strong? If my face didn't break out?

Chances are you'll answer that you'd be more attractive; therefore, more people would like you and you'd be happier. So probably your real goal isn't weight loss or strong muscles or clear skin. It is being more accepted, having better relationships, and feeling happier.

Your real goal may be having better relationships, being more accepted, and feeling happier.

31

Step 2: Focus on Your Strengths

The next question is, Will changing the way you look really help you reach your goal? That is a harder one to answer. It didn't for Tisdale. She found that her happiness depended on how she felt inside, not on how she looked outside. Even though she felt better about her body when she was thinner, she didn't feel better about herself.

Many people find this is so. They realize that changing their looks doesn't change them. But people who change their attitudes toward themselves often find that their appearance changes, too!

How can you change your feelings about yourself? Start by making a list of your strengths and skills. Are you kind? Do you have a good sense of humor? Do you like taking care of animals? Playing handball? Dancing? Do you make up great stories? Can you keep calm when others lose their cool? Write down what you like about yourself. Then think about how you might use your strengths to have more fun and build better relationships. Next, find out what others like about you (see step 3).

Step 3: Ask for the Good News

Robert Brooks, a psychologist who writes about self-esteem, says that we live in a "praise deficit" society. We're quick to point out each other's faults, but not the strengths. Because we don't often say why we like each other, many of us have little idea of what others value in us. This can lead us to misunderstand what others like about us or, worse, to wonder if we are valued at all.

How to find out the truth? Ask. Ask others what they like about you. Ask what they think are your strengths. This may feel funny, but if you ask someone you know well and really trust, you may learn some interesting things about yourself.

Asking is only the first part. You also have to accept what the person says. Echo back what you hear. If someone says, "I like you because you make me laugh," try saying back: "I hear you saying that you think I have a good sense of humor." Don't be surprised if this exercise makes you want to cry. We often don't realize that we are valued. Finding out that we are—and why—can be a moving experience.

Step 4: Tune in Your Inner Fan

If real attractiveness and happiness come from self-acceptance, then you need to build self-esteem along with muscles. One of the best ways to do this is to give yourself a good talking-to.

The emphasis here is on the word *good*. We constantly talk to ourselves. What we say matters. If we tell ourselves we're fat, we feel fat. If we tell ourselves we're ugly, we feel ugly. If we tell ourselves that no one will like us, we act in ways that keep others away.

Too often we talk to ourselves through our inner critic. The voice we use blames and scolds. It uses words like *never, bad, always*, as in: Your hair is so thin it will never look good. You ate that cookie. You're really bad. We can't get rid of the critic. If we try, we're bound to fail, because the critic is part of us. But it is only one part.

We also have an inner fan. The fan believes in us and thinks we're great! The fan looks at our problems in helpful, not hurtful, ways. It says: You have thin hair. Why don't you look through magazines for styles that will look good? You ate that cookie, but it's only one cookie. It won't make you fat, and you don't have to eat more.

When you hear the blaming critic, you need to say: Thank you for your opinion, but now I'd like to hear what the fan has to say. Then you need to let the fan come through. This takes practice. We're so used to the critic that we often don't realize that it is not the only inner voice trying to be heard.

Step 5: Beware the Put-Down Pros

It's hard to let the fan speak up when put-down pros and media hype tell us over and over that we must look a certain way to be attractive.

You need to tune into these messages before you can tune them out. If you keep your put-down meter on alert, you will become more aware of what others are saying. When the meter goes off, stop and listen. Evaluate what you are hearing. Some comments *are* helpful advice. Many are not. When you feel you're hearing from the put-down pros, remember:

■ They have their opinions, you have yours. Their opinions are not necessarily right or better than yours.

■ People are attracted to who you are, not just how you look.

■ You look your best when you let yourself be yourself, not when you try to look like someone else.

■ You look your best when you like yourself and let your good feelings show.

Friends who criticize you may really be insecure about themselves. Their comments might have more to do with their own fears than with you.

■ A girlfriend or boyfriend who demands that you look or act a certain way isn't attracted to you but to an idea of who you should be. You need and deserve friends who like you for who you are. If they don't, the problem is theirs, not yours.

■ Adults or friends who criticize you may really be insecure about themselves. Their comments might have more to do with their own fears than with you.

Step 6: Redefine Sex Appeal

If you ask adults what first attracted them to their mates, they might well mention a physical feature. But usually the loved one's hair, eyes, or smile reflected something else that was the true attraction: warmth, humor, kindness, intelligence.

Think about this yourself. What attracts you to other people? Is it only how they look? Or is it what their looks seem to say about who they are?

The most attractive people often have a style all their own. They please us because they let themselves shine through: "No matter how you look, you will be drawn together by styles, energy, and traits that reflect who you are," says **psychiatrist** John Livingstone. "There is someone for everyone."

Step 7: Don't Diet

The trouble with diets is that they don't work. They restrict foods and calories so much that we're bound to rebel. When we do, we feel like failures and the body blues get worse, not better. What's more, we will most likely gain back the weight we lost—95 percent of all dieters do.

We might gain even more. Doctors note that people who regain weight after a diet often end up weighing more than before the diet. Set point helps explain why. When we try to starve ourselves into thinness, the body goes into survival mode. It starts using calories more slowly in order to keep weight near the set point. When we eat normally again, it does more than restore our former weight: It sets our set point a bit higher to guard against future starvation. Thus each diet might *raise* our natural weight! This is only a theory, but it explains a common experience.

Research also shows that each time we lose and then regain weight, we end up with more fat and less muscle. This makes us look worse and is bad for our health. Excess fat is linked to problems like heart disease.

Your goal should be a healthy body. As noted earlier, females need a certain amount of body fat. Only a doctor can tell you if you need to lose weight to be healthy. Only a doctor or a **nutritionist** can help you develop a diet that is safe for your growing body and that will help you meet and maintain an appropriate weight.

Moderate exercise and good eating habits are enough to keep most people healthy and fit. A diet that is low in fat and allows many foods in moderation is one that can lead to a lifetime of healthy eating. And studies show that *permanent* changes in eating habits—not fad diets—are what keep weight off. We can eat cereal for supper and salads for breakfast. We can snack all day or eat three meals. It doesn't matter. What does matter is that we get enough lean, nutritious food to support our health and growth.

Step 8: Don't Eat When You Want to Cry

One thing we can do to control weight is to eat only when we are hungry, not when we are sad, lonely, angry, overtired, or depressed. Although not all people who are overweight overeat, some do. Often they eat to feel better. They "swallow their anger" or fill the emptiness inside with ice cream.

For most of us, food is associated with love, comfort, and security. As infants we were held close and cuddled when we were fed. As children we got cakes on our birthdays and, often, sweet treats for being good. Some of us even had our tears chased away by a parent's loving hug and the offer of a cookie so we wouldn't feel sad.

One thing we can do to control weight is to eat only when we are hungry, not when we are sad, lonely, angry, overtired, or depressed.

It's no wonder, then, that as teens and adults we often turn to food to ease our pain or to treat ourselves. But if we're worried about our weight, the relief may be short-lived, and the treat can turn into torture.

Weight counselors suggest that people keep food diaries to become aware of why and when they eat. Write down what you ate and how you felt at the time. If keeping notes seems too much of a hassle, try catching yourself in the act. As you're about to down that third cupcake, ask yourself: "Am I really hungry right now? What am I feeling? What may have happened to drive me to eat?"

Over time you might see some patterns. Perhaps you drown your anger at your parents with a chocolate shake.

One of the best ways to beat the body blues is to exercise. When we exercise, we do something positive for our health, bodies, and minds.

Or maybe you nibble on brownies when you're bored. Once you know your habits, you can find better ways to deal with the emotions that cause overeating. After all, a talk with a friend or a ride on your bike will cure boredom better than brownies!

Some people are **compulsive eaters.** They start eating and can't stop. They may eat huge amounts of food all at once. This is a serious problem. It is often linked to psychological troubles. If you eat like this, get help. Licensed therapists and support groups like Overeaters Anonymous can help you.

Step 9: Exercise

One of the best ways to beat the body blues is to exercise. When we exercise, we do something positive for our health, bodies, and minds. Exercise can help us feel in control and boost our self-esteem. People who regularly exercise say they become more energetic, less moody, and more relaxed—all of which help us feel better about ourselves.

Exercise can also help us control our body shape. It tones muscles and increases our **metabolism**, the rate at which the body uses calories. What's more, if you exercise, maybe you'll have less time to watch TV. Recent studies suggest that watching TV might slow down kids' metabolism!

Exercise comes in many forms. You can jog, walk, swim, bike, play a team sport, or work out with weights or an **aerobics** tape. The secret to making an exercise program stick is making it fun. Find out which sports will best help you meet your fitness goals (strength, muscle building, weight loss, or overall health). Then choose the type of exercise you think you'll like best. As you become good at it, your enjoyment will grow.

Try to exercise three times a week, for about 30 minutes each time. If you can do more, great. If you end up doing less, that's okay, too. The important thing is to do what feels good to you and to keep at it over time. And don't expect miracles. Exercise has many benefits, but it won't turn you into a movie star. Remember: You're doing this to be the very best *you* can be, not to become someone else!

Step 10: Celebrate Yourself!

"Since I've stopped worrying about losing weight, I've been having so much fun," says Kaitlin. "Like before, if a friend asked me to go for pizza, I'd go, 'No. I'm on a diet.' Then I'd get so mad at myself 'cause I really wanted to go. Now I just say, 'Sure! I'd love to.' Maybe I have some pizza, maybe I don't. But I always have a good time."

One of the worst things about the body blues is that they can make people put their lives on hold: I can't buy a bathing suit. I'm too fat. I can't get that new haircut. My ears will show. I can't ask that girl out. I'm too ugly. Too short. Too skinny . . . You know how the list goes. But we may always be short or skinny or fat. Our ears may always stick out. Should we put our lives on hold forever?

No! We deserve to have fun. We deserve to look our best. We deserve to let the people we are shine through, no matter what the inner critic or the put-down pros say. So the next time you hear that little voice saying, "You can't. You're too . . . ," answer, "Oh, yes I can!" Celebrate yourself! By valuing yourself as you are today, you can become a better you tomorrow.

Celebrate yourself! By valuing yourself as you are today, you can become a better you tomorrow.

43

A Final Word

The body blues can lead to a serious eating disorder. What starts out as an effort to control weight ends up a dangerous, even life-threatening, disease.

The most common eating disorders are **bulimia** and **anorexia nervosa.** People who have bulimia **binge** and then **purge.** They may repeat this cycle only 2 or 3 times a week or as often as 20 or more times a day. Those with anorexia starve themselves. Like bulimics, they cannot control their behavior. Even when they look like famine victims, they still see themselves as fat and do not eat.

These two disorders have much in common. More females suffer from them than males, and the disorders most often begin in the teen or young adult years. Also, both are thought to have a physical cause, although psychological stresses often play a role as well.

Anorexia and bulimia are not the only body-image-related problems teens can develop. Young athletes who want to improve performance, or boys who simply want larger muscles, may take **steroids.** These are powerful drugs. They can cause problems that range from annoying to life-threatening: acne, bad breath, mood swings, high blood pressure, and liver damage and cancers, to name just a few. Steroids can stunt growth and become addictive.

Anorexia, bulimia, and steroid use are all serious problems. If you have one of them, speak to your doctor. The sooner you are treated, the better your chances of recovery.

If You'd Like to Learn More

Organizations

The following groups provide information on eating disorders or steroids:

American Anorexia/Bulimia Association, Inc.
418 East 76th Street
New York, NY 10021

National Anorexic Aid Society, Inc.
1925 East Dublin-Granville Road
Columbus, OH 43229

Consumer Information Center
National Institute of Mental Health
Dept. 77
Pueblo, CO 81009

National Institute on Drug Abuse Hotline
1-800-662-HELP

Overeaters Anonymous
Box 92870
Los Angeles, CA 90009
1-800-743-8703

Books and Movies

Books and movies can help us understand our feelings better. Here are some that deal with body image.

Blubber, by Judy Blume (New York: Bradbury Press, 1974). This novel focuses on the abusive and cruel behavior that often takes place among children. It is about an overweight fifth-grader who is tormented and nicknamed "Blubber" by her classmates.

Changing Bodies, Changing Lives, by Ruth Bell (New York: Random House, 1988). This is a thorough, straightforward book about sexual development and its impact on our bodies and relationships.

Staying Fat for Sarah Byrnes, by Chris Crutcher (New York: Greenwillow Books, 1993). This novel by an award-winning writer tells the story of how an overweight boy and a disfigured girl learn to open themselves to friendship and let their true selves show.

Roxanne (1987): In this comic take-off on the classic *Cyrano de Bergerac*, Steve Martin plays a man who thinks that the woman he loves (Daryl Hannah) could never love him because of the length of his nose.

What's Eating You? (Charleston, WV: Cambridge Educational, 1992). This half-hour video on body image provides information on beauty, nutrition, dieting, and exercise. It includes helpful suggestions.

Glossary/Index

aerobics: 41 Exercise that benefits the heart.
anorexia nervosa: 44 An eating disorder in which people starve themselves.
body blues: 6 The belief that you will not be liked or accepted because of how you look.
body image: 8 Your inner picture of how you look.
binge: 44 To eat an unusually large amount of food in a short time.
bulimia: 44 An eating disorder in which people binge and purge at least twice a week and often much more than that.
compulsive eaters: 40 People who cannot stop themselves from eating huge amounts at once.
culture: 9 The customs and beliefs that characterize a society or part of a society.
genes: 25 Material in the body that is inherited and determines the traits a person exhibits.
heredity: 14 The traits passed on through the genes from one's ancestors.
inner critic: 5 An inner voice that finds fault with the way you look, feel, and act.
metabolism: 41 The rate at which the body uses calories.
nutritionist: 37 Someone specially trained to help people create diets that meet their health needs.
predispose: 26 Make more likely to happen.
psychiatrist: 36 A medical doctor who studies how people feel, act, and think, and who treats people who are emotionally troubled.
psychologist: 5 Someone specially trained to understand human behavior and emotions and to help people who are emotionally troubled.
puberty: 13 The time in life when a person is first able to reproduce sexually.
purge: 44 To eliminate food or calories by vomiting, fasting, over-exercising, or using laxatives or diuretics.
scoliosis: 9 Curvature of the spine.
self-esteem: 16 Your confidence in and satisfaction with yourself.
set point: 28 The body's natural weight. If you are not ill, are eating a healthy diet, and are getting moderate exercise, the body will tend to stay at its natural weight.
sex hormones: 13 The chemicals that govern sex characteristics such as facial hair in men and menstrual cycles in women.
steroids: 45 Powerful drugs derived from male sex hormones.